More Hours In My Day

Emilie Barnes

HARVEST HOUSE PUBLISHERS
Eugene, Oregon 97402

Cover Design: Larry Smith & Associates, Inc., Atlanta

MORE HOURS IN MY DAY

Copyright © 1982, 1989, 1994 by Harvest House Publishers
Eugene, Oregon 97402

Library of Congress Cataloging-in-Publication Data

Barnes, Emilie
        More hours in my day / Emilie Barnes.
            p.   cm.
        Rev. ed. of: More hours in my day.   1982.
        Includes bibliographical references.
        ISBN 1-56507-233-2
        1. Time management—Religious aspect—Christianity.   2. Women—Time
    management.   3. Home economics.   4. Women—Conduct of life.   5. Women—
    Religious life.   I. Barnes, Emilie.   More hours in my day.   II. Title.
    BV4598.5.B37   1994
    640—dc20   94-6866
                                                                                 CIP

Printed in the United States of America.

94   95   96   97   98   99   00   01   —   10   9   8   7   6   5   4   3   2

This book is dedicated to my husband, Bob, who has loved me for over 39 years. He has continued to encourage and teach me in the Lord and in our home. I thank him for making it possible to keep our home my priority and still letting me be me in the ministry of "More Hours in My Day" seminars.

I thank my mother, who is at home with the Lord, for the domestic-engineering education she gave me as I was growing up. And I thank her for seeing the wonderful qualities in Bob and for allowing me to marry him at 17 years of age.

Bob has motivated me to organize and be creative in our home and with our children, Brad and Jenny.

Together we complement each other, all because of Bob's faithfulness to our Lord and his honest and manly spirit. He is truly a man after God's own heart. And because of that we are together in a full-time ministry of teaching God's principles to those whom God brings into our lives through "More Hours in My Day" seminars.

Contents

Introduction

❧ Part 3 ❧
More Hours...for Resource Savers

❧ Part 4 ❧
More Hours...for Family and Friends

❧ Part 5 ❧
More Hours...for Your Children

Introduction

What you are about to read is the second revision of *More Hours in My Day*. It's important for you to know this because when I first wrote the book in 1982, it was everything in the whole wide world that I knew. Today, over 14 books later, as I speak to over 8000 women each year at conferences, retreats, and the popular "More Hours in My Day Seminars," I find women more hungry to be organized and creative homemakers than ever before. I've learned a lot in these past years as I've matured and as women have graciously shared with me their hearts and frustrations.

As I cross the country from coast to coast over a dozen times a year, I've come to know women's hearts of pain. I've also come to see hearts of joy released as women apply the principles in this book and in others I have written. Lives have been changed, homes united, home businesses started, other ministries begun, children taught, and Christians revived and renewed and reborn.

Today more than ever before women are crying out for more hours in their day. God has given us 24 hours—should He have given 29? We would fill those up as well. When we take those God-given hours and apply the godly priorities and principles to our lives, we will find that God redeems the hours and bless us with peace and contentment.

The new *More Hours in My Day* is chock-full of all the creative ideas the Lord has taught me since the beginning of our ministry in 1982. I thank God for so many women across America who have shared with me their "more hours" experiences.

In the first chapter I share with you my life story— how God can take ordinary women and design them into women who make a difference in the lives of people around them for His glory. Yes, I am an older woman teaching younger women (Titus 2:3-5), and I'm proud to do just that.

May God touch your "more hours" as you apply the teachings of this book.

Lovingly,

Emilie

Part

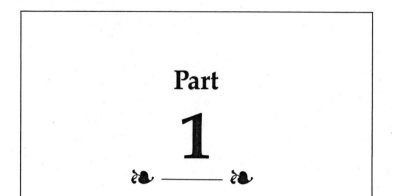

1

More Hours...
for You

1

A Woman Designed

You created my inmost being;
you knit me together in my mother's womb.
I praise you because I am
fearfully and wonderfully made.

Psalm 139:13,14 NIV

ह‍ — ह‍

I rene was a Jewish girl born in Brooklyn, New York, the oldest of five children. Her mother died during the birth of Irene's baby sister. And Papa, a gifted tailor, died a few years later, leaving teenaged Irene to raise her brothers and sisters. Jobs and money were in California, so the young family headed for Hollywood to make a life for themselves.

As a young adult, Irene designed and sewed tennis dresses for movie stars in the early 1920s. She worked hard to support herself and her brothers and sisters. At 29 she met Otto Klein, a 40-year-old chef for Paramount Studios. Irene married Otto in 1930.

Irene badly wanted children, but Otto wouldn't hear of it. As a German Jew and a veteran of World War I, Otto had barely escaped the war with his life. He wasn't about to bring children into such an angry world. Twice Irene became pregnant and twice he forced her into abortions. When she became pregnant a third time, Irene refused to terminate the pregnancy. In July 1934, a beautiful son, Edmund Francis Klein, was born to Otto and Irene. Four years later, on April 12, 1938, Emilie Marie Klein was born. Otto adored his baby daughter, but his young son Edmund became the abused victim of a father filled with hatred from abuse he himself had suffered as a child.

Otto was a creative and artistic man. As an orphan in Vienna he was placed in the palace to be a kitchen helper. His exceptional ability gained him training by the finest chefs in Europe, and Otto became an expert Viennese chef. He escaped war-torn Europe, traveling first to New York and then to Hollywood. There he became a chef to movie stars—Clark Gable, Mickey Rooney, Lana Turner, Greta Garbo, Mario Lanza, Douglas Fairbanks, Judy Garland, and many more. Yet deep inside this successful man was a little boy still hurting from the loss of his parents.

Otto turned to alcohol to escape his pain, jeopardizing his career and his family. Otto's drinking fueled his angry perfectionism, resulting in violent outbursts at the shortcomings of his coworkers, wife, and children.

Irene's fear for the safety of herself and her children smothered her fun-loving, sanguine temperament. Edmund stored his anger for his abusive father, releasing it later in rebellion. And Emilie—that's me—became a very bashful, quiet child.

I have only a few happy memories of my father. When I was nine years old we moved to Long Beach, California, where Daddy managed a restaurant called Ormando's. He would take me on walks along the beach and we would fish off the pier. He gave me a beautiful blue bicycle on my tenth birthday.

Daddy lost his job at Ormando's due to his temper and drinking problem. My brother, Edmund, who was almost 14 at the time, began his years of rebellion. Then Daddy became very ill. He refused to listen to his doctors. Instead he got mad at them and demanded that they make him well.

Because of my father, the emotional thermometer in our home was almost always on high. It was my job to try to keep peace, and I was able to cool Daddy's temper at times. He adored me and never abused me. But I hurt inside because of what he did to my mother and brother. I suffered from nightmares, and I wished Daddy would die and relieve us of the control he held over us with his hot temper.

Daddy didn't let Mama cook very often because she didn't meet his gourmet standards. But she was also a great cook. Her corned beef cabbage rolls and other Jewish meals are a delicious memory. Occasionally Mama and Daddy would prepare a meal together, and I would sit on the drain board watching and learning. Those were happy days for me—probably because Daddy wasn't drinking on those days.

The summer after my eleventh birthday my wish came true. Daddy died and we were released from his bondage. I cried as I looked toward heaven wondering about the afterlife. But I quickly pushed those thoughts out of my mind. Mama was now a single parent with two children to care for. Being unemployed and uninsured, Daddy left us with hospital and doctor bills.

My aunt and uncle kept us afloat financially and helped my mother open up a small dress shop in Long Beach. We lived in a three-room apartment behind the store—kitchen, living room, and one bedroom. It was perfect for our needs. We gave Edmund the bedroom and Mama and I slept together in a Murphy bed in the living room. Mama gave me the responsibility of caring for those three rooms while she ran the dress shop. I painted the whole apartment myself, even though I had never painted in my life. I decorated the walls and, with help from Mama, made curtains, tablecloths, and chair covers. I planted flowers in our window box and kept the bathroom and kitchen spotless. Under Mama's direction I prepared the meals and washed the laundry.

Mama was a Proverbs 31 woman and didn't even know it. She was a hard worker, often working at the shop late into the night. She watched for bargains in order to make our money go farther. Together we transformed our simple apartment into a haven of peace.

My brother shattered our peaceful home, making it a home filled with stress and worry. His teachers called, the principal called, and then Edmund was kicked out of school. Several times the police called Mama in the early-morning hours, telling her that Edmund was in jail. Mama and I would get up, wait for the city bus, and travel to the police station to identify him. Poor Mama was heartbroken over her son. Finally Edmund enlisted in the Marines, and a few years later he was married.

Mama was able to work us out of debt, so we moved to a larger apartment away from the store. By this time I was in complete control of our apartment—washing, ironing, and planning meals. I was also going to school, working in our dress shop, and traveling with Mama to the garment district in Los Angeles once a month to buy dresses. My mother had trained me well.

During the years following Daddy's death, we became active in our local Jewish temple. On Wednesdays after public school I attended Hebrew school taught by the rabbi. At 15 I was confirmed at the temple, and my family was proud of their little Jewish girl. But my confirmation didn't bring peace to my heart, and I still didn't have the answer to my questions about life after death.

At age 16 I attended a modeling class at the Wilma Hastings Modeling School. It was there that I met Esther, the most talented, beautiful, and natural model in our class. Esther later went to New York and became a high-fashion model, appearing on the cover of several fashion magazines.

Esther stayed with me a week that summer. We went to the beach, worked in the dress shop, and played "fashion show." One evening we went to the movies and there met Bill Barnes. Bill wanted to date Esther, but Esther and I had made an agreement that we would only double date. Esther told Bill that he would have to find a date for her girlfriend Emilie. Bill's identical twin, Bob, owed him a favor, so Bob Barnes became my blind date.

I was immediately attracted to Bob by his deep tan, faded denim pants, white shirt, and saddle shoes. He was a mature college student, athletic and strong. He opened the doors for me, displayed gracious manners, and carried himself with an air of gentleness. There was something very different about him.

Esther and I had been experimenting with cigarettes and planned to smoke in front of these college men to show them how mature we were. When Esther offered me a cigarette I heard a voice inside me say, "Don't do it!" So I refused, and was I ever glad. Later we discovered that Bill and Bob didn't smoke, and I wanted Bob to be impressed with me.

I was shy, bashful, and very quiet during our blind date. I figured that if I didn't talk a lot I wouldn't say the wrong thing and reveal my age. I didn't want to blow it with Bob Barnes.

I was absolutely shocked when Bob called me for a real date. On the day of our date I cleaned the house, baked cookies, washed and set my hair, polished my nails, and washed and ironed clothes. I prepared the atmosphere by lighting candles and boiling cinnamon sticks on the stove to give the apartment a homey aroma. I wanted everything to be perfect—even the things he wouldn't see when he came to pick me up.

Being the homemaker of the century, I won the heart of my man—except for one area. I was a Jewish girl and Bob was a committed Christian. Mama really liked Bob, a clean-cut gentleman. But my aunts and uncles were outraged that Mama allowed me to date a Gentile—worse yet, a "dyed-in-the-wool Baptist," as they called him. "You are making a big mistake, Irene," they told Mama. "He'll never amount to anything. He's not good enough for our Emilie. They'll have a miserable life. She's too young, so send him away. Better yet, send her away."

Even though I didn't know it at the time, God was in control. By the time I was 16 our relationship was growing deep and serious. Bob's family was praying for me during those dating months as Bob patiently read the Scriptures to me, took me to church, directed me to messages by Billy Graham, and introduced me to his Christian friends. One verse that pierced my heart was John 14:6: "Jesus answered, 'I am the way and the truth and the life. No one comes to the Father except through me' " (NIV). I asked myself, *Is Jesus the Messiah our people are waiting for?*

Then I read Romans 6:23: "The wages of sin is death, but the gift of God is eternal life in Christ Jesus our Lord" (NIV). *Eternal life—is that the answer to an 11-year-old's questions about life after death? Can I have life forever and ever by believing in Jesus Christ and receiving Him into my heart? Is dying merely a change of address from earth to heaven?*

Bob gently guided me into the family of God. One night, in the quietness of my room, I knelt, opened the door of my heart, and invited the Lord Jesus—Messiah Yeshua—into my life. I asked Him to change me and give me a heart ready to serve Him. I asked Him to take control of me and guide me on a path that would please Him.

Having cleared the only hurdle between us, I wanted to marry Bob Barnes and build a healthy, happy, spiritual home free from abuse and anger; a home with harmony, love, and the fragrance of Jesus. I knew we could have that kind of home, even though the path would be rocky at times. But Bob and I were committed to the common goal of serving the Lord and serving each other. We could survive with God's help.

The criticism from my family grew strong, especially after we announced our engagement. My aunt and uncle offered to send me to one of the best finishing schools in Europe, buy me a car and a wardrobe, and provide me an unlimited expense account if I would not marry Bob. But my heart now belonged to God and to Bob. I had already received the greatest gift—God's Son, Messiah Jesus—with no strings attached. I told my aunt and uncle that I loved them, but I was going to marry Bob and establish a Christian home.

In September 1955, Bob (age 22) and I (age 17) were married. Yes, my relatives' hearts were broken. Family pressure was heavy on Mama, who agreed to sign for me to marry at my young age. But, thank God, I was not disowned or "buried" as some Jews are when they marry outside the faith. My family didn't think our marriage would last more than a few months. But we had a loving God guiding our hearts and lives.

Shortly after our wedding I began my senior year of high school and Bob began his first year of teaching. I wasn't much older than his students. Bob helped me with term papers, signed my report cards, and attended senior activities with me. I received the homemaker of the year award, starred in the senior play, and served as student body secretary as the only married student at Long Beach Poly High School.

After graduation I kept house, worked in the dress shop, and later took a job with a bank. I wanted a family, but Bob felt we should wait until we could afford a house and he was secure in his school district. Three years later our daughter, Jennifer Christine, was born.

Just a few months after Jennifer arrived we became parents to three more children. My brother Edmund's wife left for the market one day and never returned home, walking out on her husband and three pre-school children—Tawney, Keri, and Kevin. We have seen her only once in over 37 years, and she has never contacted her children. Edmund became very depressed and was unable to care for his children. Bob and I felt the children needed love and stability, so we asked Edmund if he would let us take them into our home. We soon became legal guardians for Tawney, Keri, and Kevin.

Mothering four children under the age of four was an exhausting job. I cooked, baked, cleaned, washed, ironed, and did everything I could to create a loving home for our family. I made all the children's clothes, plus my own. Whenever Bob wasn't refereeing football or basketball games he was home by 4:00 P.M., which was a great help to me. I was happy that my childhood responsibilities had equipped me with the tools I needed—another proof that God works all things together for His purposes.

A few weeks after Edmund's children came, I discovered that I was pregnant. I was so sick with number five that it was difficult to carry on with the other four. One day I was so sick that I took the four kids into the backyard, spread a blanket on the grass, and passed out. I didn't care if they ate dirt or snails while I slept; I wouldn't need to feed them lunch.

Another day three-year-old Keri got into some paint cans in our neighbor's garage. I found her covered head to toe in red oil-based paint. After stripping her clothes and cleaning her with paint remover and a warm bath, I put us both down for a nap. Fifteen minutes later she was back into the paint again.

In May 1960 our son, Bradley Joe Barnes, was born, giving us five children under five years of age—and I was only 21. My mother was still running the dress shop so she was unable to help me. Bob was a great help, but he had a profession, night classes, and a part-time refereeing job. So raising the children was my baby in more ways than one. I survived the next few years until Edmund remarried. His wife had two children, so when Edmund's three went back to him they had a family of seven.

By this time Mama's business had faltered and she filed for bankruptcy. She lost what little she had and slipped into a deep depression. She was in her early sixties with no home, no job, and no future. We invited Mama to live with us until she could reorganize her life. Mama's visit turned out to be another step in the path of God's plan. Being in our home, she attended church with us and the Spirit of God touched her heart. In 1964 Mama invited the Messiah into her life. At this writing she is the only one of my family members to come into the Christian family. But I'm not giving up on my family. John 14:14 says: "If you ask me for anything in my name, I will do it" (TEV). I'm trusting our Lord for each of my family members, and He will answer.

Bob and I continued to raise our family, and as I grew up with the children we learned much together. Bob and I were committed to God, family, love, goals, and raising responsible adults. I worked at being industrious, creative, and very organized in our family life, which gave me more hours in my day.

At age 29 I became the first chairwoman of the Newport Beach Christian Women's Club. That year I was asked to speak to over 800 women at a conference in Palm Springs. I was so naive and absolutely scared to death. But the response to my testimony overwhelmed me. Other chairwomen asked me to speak at their meetings. Rose Tiffany, a long-time Christian friend who supported me in prayer that day, answered, "She'll come," and started booking dates. Since that time I have spoken to several hundred Christian Women's Clubs.

In 1971 we moved from Newport Beach to Riverside, California. I was 33 years old. Our years in Newport Beach had gained us some very close friends and church relationships. We had grown spiritually so much at Mariners Church that it was hard to begin again. By this time

Mama had moved into a senior citizens' building. She attended Bible studies, met others her age, and grew through the great teaching she received.

Our move to Riverside wasn't easy for me. I was homesick for our friends. It was during this time that I met Florence Littauer. We had much in common as speakers, and our husbands encouraged us to write a seminar for women. In the Spring of 1973 Florence and I taught our first "Feminar" to only a handful of women. But it was a beginning. God was paving the way for our ministries. Florence founded C.L.A.S.S. (Christian Leaders and Speakers' Seminar), and Bob and I founded the "More Hours in My Day" seminar. Florence has written over 20 books and speaks to thousands of women all over the world. We are just two ordinary women open to God's leading, with two supportive, encouraging husbands cheering us on.

As you advance through this book, you will begin to see how important it is to have a plan of organization. And as you work through that plan, the plan will work for you.

Eighty-five percent of our stress is caused by disorganization. The benefits of order in our lives are great: Stress is relieved, hours redeemed, and joy regained.

May your life be blessed as you begin that plan and as you are given more hours in your busy day.

2

Me, Get Organized?

God created man in his own image,
in the image of God he created him;
male and female he created them.

Genesis 1:27, NIV

❧ —— ❧

Over the years I have received countless letters from women who want to know how to get organized. Either through coaxing from their husbands, children, friends, or clergy, they have begun to realize that they could be more effective if they somehow could get organized.

That word *organized* means many things to many people. For some it might be putting their papers in colored file folders, for some it means putting all their seasonings in ABC order, for some it means a clean house, and for others it means being able to retrieve papers that have been stored away.

Even after writing 14 books with a combined total of over 3000 pages dealing with the single topic of organization, I'm not sure I have covered all bases for all women. However, I have found the following to be basic requirements when a person wants to become organized.

- *Start with you.* What is it about you that causes you to be disorganized? I find that organized people have a calmness and serenity about them that disorganized people don't have. Search your own self to see what is causing all that confusion. See if you can't get rid of that clutter first before you move on. In some cases you may need to meet with your clergy or even a professional counselor who can help you unravel the causes of this disorganization. I didn't say it was going to be easy to get organized.

- *Keep it simple.* There are many programs available, but choose one that's simple. You don't want to spend all your time keeping up charts and graphs.

- *Make sure everything has a designated place.* One of our sayings is "Don't put it down, put it away." Another is "Don't pile it, file it." If there is no place for stuff to go, it's going to get piled. That's one thing you want to prevent—piles.

- *Store like items together.* Bob has his gardening supplies and tools together. I have my laundry items in one place, my bill-paying tools in one area, my prayer basket and its tools together, my cups/saucers, my drinking glasses, and my dinnerware all in their general area. You don't want to spend time going from here to there getting ready for your tasks. Put them in one place.

- *Even though you are neat you may not be organized.* I tell my women to use notebook organizers and that there are two things they need to remember. One, write it down; and two, read it. It doesn't do you much good if you write down that birthday date or that appointment on your calendar and yet you forget both because you didn't read it on the calendar. Remember to write *and* read.

- *Get rid of all items you don't use.* Read chapter 14 on "Total Mess to Total Rest" in this book. It will give you great help in getting rid of all the unused stuff.

- *Invest in the proper tools.* In order to be organized you need proper tools: bins, hooks, racks, containers, lazy Susans, etc.

- *Involve the whole family.* Learn to delegate jobs and responsibilities to other members of the family. My Bob takes care of all the repairs. When something is broken, he is Mr. Fix-It. Depending upon the ages of the children, you will need to tailor-make their chores. Also, change off frequently so they don't get bored. Don't do something yourself that another member of the family can do.

- *Keep master lists.* I've learned to use my three-ring binder, my 3" x 5" file cards, and journals to keep track of all our stuff. Many of these techniques are woven throughout my various books. You may think you'll never forget that you loaned that CD to Brad or that video to Christine, but you will. Write it down and keep the list in a place where you cannot overlook it. (In *Survival For Busy Women* I have some charts for doing this activity.)

- Continually reevaluate your system. Nothing is written in concrete. It can be changed. See how other people do things, read a book to gather ideas, evaluate your own system. Change when it's not working.

- Use a lot of labels and signs. If containers, bins, drawers, and shelves aren't labeled, the family won't be able to spot where things go. I have also used color coding to help identify items belonging to various members of the family: blue for Bevan, red for Chad, and purple for Christine.

I use a fine-point paint pen very effectively to label clothes, glass and plastic jars, and wooden items. (Don't use water-base pens—they will not last very long.) You can also purchase a label maker for around six dollars at a variety store.

Where to start? Start with these suggestions. Get them under control, and then you can move into more specific areas.

3

Women Prepared or Ill-Prepared

*Some will use gold or silver
or precious stones in building
on the foundation. Others will use
wood or grass or straw.*

1 Corinthians 3:12, TEV

୬ —— ୬

D o you remember hearing as a child the story of the three little pigs who wanted to build homes for themselves? The first little pig liked to play all the time, so he quickly built a house of straw and then went to play. The second little pig liked to rest, so he quickly built his house of sticks, then took a snooze. The third little pig was a hard worker and a planner—he wanted to build the best house he could, so he built his house out of bricks. Remember the rest of the story about the big, bad wolf who huffed and puffed and blew the straw and stick houses down without any problem? But when he got to the house of bricks, no amount of huffing and puffing could blow the strong brick house down. We can learn much from that story.

The past several decades relate much to the structure of the pigs' homes. Compare what we were in the fifties to what we are today. I know the fifties well because that was my era. We believed in school, marriage, home, children, the American family, and prayer—good, solid, wholesome tradition. As we moved into the sixties, we experienced rebellion, protest, riots, flower children, "do my own thing"—the "me generation" it was called. The seventies found us with a strong women's liberation movement, careers, more "me" independence, a higher divorce rate, and women taking traditional men's roles. The eighties found us to be super-hyper women; supermoms; stressed-out, materialistic yuppies with the perfect everything: car, house, children, husband, job, vacation, acrylic nails, car phones, Guess jeans, and so on. It has been a "do it ourselves" and "we can do it" generation.

The nineties have found us exhausted. As we evaluate the past, we realize it didn't give us the peace and happiness that we wanted. Instead we find hurt, agony, grief, unhappiness, more divorce, alcohol abuse, drug dependence, increased teen suicide, absent moms, AIDS, child abuse, and so on. We've opened our eyes to what we have done in the past. Now we see the need to heal and change. Many communities are aware of the helps needed—from diet centers to drug rehab centers to hospitals. There are support groups of all kinds. We're talking about issues such as incest, adult children of alcoholics, cults, Satan worship—and the list goes on. You name it and we've done it. We look back and see what we did wrong. Yes, we've come full circle. The approaches of the sixties, seventies, and eighties didn't work—divorce is 50 percent in first marriages and 70 percent in second marriages; drugs, AIDS, physical abuse, and child-care centers are much more prevalent than in the fifties.

Women Rebuilding Our Dream House

> "Do yourself a favor and learn all you can;
> then remember what you've learned and you
> will prosper" (Proverbs 19:8, TEV).

Today we are returning to a new traditionalism. We are looking at our past mistakes and beginning to see what we can do to correct them. To become the women that God uniquely created, yes, we're going back to tradition—but we will do it in a new way. We'll take on the mystique of the feminine woman, being a lady for whom men will open doors—not the "too-tired-for-sex" woman, but the woman who is beautiful inside with the charm that desires and is desired.

How are we going to do this? By changing our values from straw and sticks to gold and silver and by building a strong foundation of faith in God's Word.

Women, we are the mortar that holds together our homes and families. We set the thermostat in our homes. Proverbs 14:1 homes are made by the wisdom of women but are destroyed by foolishness. Yes, we've been foolish in some areas; we've grown and learned from that, and now we're ready to commit ourselves to making positive changes.

In *Survival for Busy Women* (Harvest House Publishers), I talk about the importance of setting goals and how to do that. Is it your goal to be at home? Do you still need help with finances? Okay, set that goal: I'd like to be at home full-time within six months or one year. Always determine a time or date when you want to reach your goal.

Our typist, Sheri Torelli, has two children and a fire-fighter husband, Tim, who works for the Riverside City Fire Department. Sheri had been a church secretary for five years, continually feeling guilty that she wasn't able to be at home during her children's preschool years. Sheri needed to work—especially during the time when Tim was out of work preparing for and then applying and training for what is now his profession. Sheri's goal was to be an "at-home woman," but it wasn't until she put a time limit to that goal that it finally happened. She now has a personal typing service in her home and is spending less time typing, plus is making more money. She is able to run her home, family, and business successfully. God has honored and blessed her heart's desire. She also has time to teach a women's Bible study in her home and do many of the things she has always wanted to do.

My friend Linda Smith has her teaching credential, and yet she's made her choice to stay home. Her husband, Greg, had open-heart surgery, and with two teenage children they needed extra finances. What should Linda do? Take a teaching job? As a family, they were committed to Linda being an "at-home woman." So Linda put her creative juices to work and started selling special gourmet desserts that she had made for her friends at dinner parties and had received compliments about how wonderful the desserts were. She sells them to restaurants in their area. Then during the holidays she makes an absolutely delicious fruitcake. Now I *hate* fruitcake, but I will admit I can overdose on Linda's. I've talked her into calling it the "I Hate Fruitcake" fruitcake. She sold 800 fruitcakes last Christmas, and people from all over order her fruitcakes.

Nancy, a single parent of two children, decided she just couldn't handle not being available to her children. She developed a computer-processing business in her home. She also did editing and proofreading. She started by putting a small ad in her local paper and in her phone book. God honored her heart and she is able to make a nice living at home so she can now be with her children.

Women, we can do whatever we want to do. I've seen women become very creative when there is a need. We seem able to rise to the occasion every time.

Several years ago I was in a cute country shop in southern California. At the entry of the store was the greatest standing "welcome goose" made of wood, painted, with a bow around his neck. I really loved the goose but debated about paying 40 dollars for such a friendly goose. Somehow I just couldn't go home without him. He was excited about adorning our front porch. Everyone loved him and asked where we got that adorable goose. Carolyn, a mother of three boys, had been asking for prayer at my Bible study group for a job for her husband and some finances to cover the living commitments of food, housing, and clothing for the family. Carolyn is talented and artistic. She commented when she saw the welcome goose, "Gary and I could do something like that." "Well, why don't you?" I asked. With a bit of wood, their own pattern, and paint, Carolyn and Gary created their own welcome goose which sold like hotcakes. They added many other woodwork items and now have a mail-order business called "The Country Carpenter" out of their home. Carolyn organizes two craft shows each year where over 50 other "women at home" present their talents. Might I add, they do very, very well. The 40-dollar investment I made was well worth it, and I can't help believing that God led me to buy that goose just for Gary and Carolyn.

I'll never forget the day Bob and I arrived at a church in southern California to present our holiday seminar. The committee was there to welcome us in red sweatshirts with appliqued Christmas trees on the front. The trees were adorned with adorable little buttons of all sizes and shapes. A tiny bell jingled at the top of each tree. I was so impressed with their creativity. These committee women made the sweatshirts a project and together they worked to make our seminar something special. From that seminar, women who saw these unique shirts wanted to order one for themselves. Debbie Carpenter, the designer, sold over 80 shirts that year and from that has created other designs. She now has a very nice business in her home and helps to supplement their income.

Sue Gregg, the coauthor of our cookbooks, attended a Feminar that Florence Littauer and I gave years ago. I did a workshop on nutrition which triggered Sue's interest because of a need to help her prediabetic husband, Rich, and to deal with other health problems in their family. Sue, a home economist, began to delve into books. Today Sue has a business in her home and has written over ten cookbooks—all with healthy, delicious, and nutritious recipes. With today's interest in health and weight control, all her recipes are low-fat, high-fiber, and quick and easy. So you can see how successful Sue's "woman-at-home" business is.

I could go on and on with all the women I know who began a business from a need for extra finances. *Entrepreneur Magazine* has a catalog of over 227 hot money-making ideas. This can be received by writing to *Entrepreneur*, P.O. Box 19787, Irvine, CA 92713-9787.

More Hours in My Day came from a need. I was teaching a Bible study in our home when the women asked how I did it all—home, children, church, Bible study, Shaklee business in my home, plus a lot of entertaining. My secret and key was that I had a plan and I worked my plan of organization. Because of their need, I scheduled a workshop in our home and 40 women showed up. I was overwhelmed. I scheduled another the next month and the same thing happened. Pretty soon women's ministry groups in churches began to call me to come and present a seminar in their church. A need was being met. Today we find ourselves in a full-time ministry. Bob closed his mobile-home company over ten years ago and we now work together doing five different seminars all over the country. We've been on national television, "Focus on the Family," and many other radio and interview programs. God lifted up our ministry and has provided the finances for us to live by working together in our home. Our children are now grown and married with grandchildren. We are loving and enjoying the time we spend with women, plus our family life.

Mix up your creative mortar and ask God what you can do to survive in the situation where you find yourself. Eighty-five percent of new businesses are started by women out of their homes.

Mary Kay Cosmetics is an excellent example. Mary Kay started her business with strong priorities and teaches them to her sales force: God—family—career.

Success? You bet—it's open in many areas to *you*, too!

Women—The Heart of the Home

My mother was a beautiful example of how the woman is the heartbeat of her home. When I was six years old my mother made me a green-and-white gingham dress with puffy sleeves, a full gathered skirt with pockets, and white heart buttons. She had a treadle Singer sewing machine. I loved to watch the rhythm of Mama's touch with her feet to make it sew. I loved that dress. It fit so perfectly—the skirt twirled just right, and it had a nice big hem in it so I could wear it for a long time.

My mother was quite a seamstress—her father had been a tailor in Brooklyn, New York, and he had to have perfection in his garments. So my dress was well-made. At first I could only wear the dress for special occasions, and absolutely could not play in it.

One of my favorite times as a little girl was when my aunt and uncle came to visit us. I got to wear my green gingham dress. This one Sunday they were late in arriving and I got tired of waiting and went out to play—only to slip and fall into a nice pile of dog toot. My dress was all I could think of. I ran home smelling very bad. Mama was great. She pulled off my dress, washed me and the dress, and assured me the dress would be fine. The episode took the newness out of that dress. Soon the green gingham dress became a school dress. I grew and the hem had to be let down. Mama sewed a band of rickrack over the hemline so it wouldn't look as if it had been altered. I was to change my dress after school. I always wanted to wear that dress, so Mama made me a new one for a best dress in the same style and a different fabric. But it just wasn't the same as my green gingham dress.

I was growing, and my favorite dress—now with three rows of rickrack—became too short to wear. Mama said it would make a fine play dress with slacks underneath. So I wore it on Saturdays to ride my bike down to the beach. By now I was eight years old. I finally had to give my green gingham dress up to the rag box.

My mother taught me how to sew, and one of my first projects was making an apron. Out came the green gingham dress from the rag box. We cut off the gathered skirt, added a waistband and ties (pockets were already there), and presto—the dress became an apron. There was still some fabric left over, and with this Mama and I made pot holders. I loved that apron, and Mama and I both wore it proudly as she taught me how to cook and clean. The pockets were big and handy to put in tidbits of trash as I cleaned each little room. What with cooking and cleaning, the apron began to get stained and a bit tattered. Unfortunately, even aprons are outgrown after a time, and back into the rag box it went. It reappeared later, however, torn into pieces. The soft fabric made fine cloths for dusting and wiping up. One day I saw my gingham dress swishing across the floor in a rag mop. Mama made our mops out of old rags, and they worked so well. The white heart buttons popped up on several dresses after that and on flannel nighties. After years of continued use, I still have two of those heart buttons, 44 years later.

Heart is created by teaching, delegating, and being there. We need to be there for our families, such as I was able to when Jenny got a splinter, had a fever, tried out for the swim team, was rejected by friends, had hair that didn't fall right, broke up with a boyfriend, and planned her wedding.

Mama was there when I fell in the toot. After my father died, she was still there working in the dress shop doing alterations, and I was in the back learning. She was great on praise and being positive. She made me believe I could do it, and I did. The negative person is never a winner.

My mother became a single parent after my father died. She truly worked far into the night, and during all her years until she died at age 78, she remained the heart of our home. Through all the abuse, alcohol-related problems, low finances, and anger in our home, Mama remained the soft, gentle-spirited woman. During her later years she lived in a senior-citizen building in a tiny, efficient apartment. Yet she had a wreath of flowers on her front door and a few fresh daisies or pansies on the table, and she always had a cup of tea ready for anyone who knocked.

What can we do to repair the brokenness of our homes, hearts, health, marriage, relationships, and children? We can begin by looking at the 8760 hours we have each year and reducing the 70 percent of stress in our lives that is caused by disorganization. If we sleep an average of eight hours per day, that equals 2920 hours a year. We then work about 2000 hours, which gives us 2700 hours of time to wash; iron; plan and prepare food; clean; attend Little League, soccer games, music recitals, and doctor appointments; help with homework; and watch television. Thirty-seven hours a week is what it takes to accomplish our domestic chores. If we find we have to work outside our homes, how can we be there to do all that? There is no time left for us, or for any interaction with our family.

Much of your hope for coping is in the remainder of this book. You can go from "Total Mess to Total Rest" in 15 minutes a day.

Our survival lies in three areas: 1. *Delegation*—Women, we can't do it alone. Supermom must go out the window. Call a family meeting and share with them your need for help and how they can help you. I know your family will come through. Prepare ahead of time a list of areas in which they can help to relieve the stress from your life. 2. *Dialogue*—Continue to share your stress feelings and allow your family to share with you. As busy as we all are, it is important to communicate back and forth about our feelings concerning teachers, schoolwork, friends, and (especially) God. 3. *Interaction*—There is much we can teach our children as we work side by side. When the children bake cookies with me, or as we make a salad, mow the lawn, wash a car, clean the bathroom, change the linens, rake leaves, and shovel snow together, we are a team. It is amazing what I found out about my children and their feelings as we worked together. I was there—the available one for them to dump on. In turn, they learned how to work, and many times our conversations were turned in spiritual directions.

Women, we are the remodelers, the harmonizers of our homes. We are a country of broken homes, broken hearts, and broken health. Staying married today is more of a challenge than getting married. To keep the flame of love alive takes creative work. Several things need to happen:

1. *We must be willing to surrender our egos to the needs of the other person.* Ephesians 5:21 (NIV) says, "Submit to one another out of reverence for Christ." My friend Jane told me with tears in her eyes that her husband wanted her to pack his lunch every day. "I won't do that for him," she cried. "I'm tired. I do everything around the house, attend to my three girls, and work as well. Let him do it himself if he wants a sack lunch so bad."

My comment to her was, "If the Lord were to ask you to pack Him a lunch, would you do it?"

"Well, of course I would," Jane snapped.

"Then tonight before you go to bed, pack a lunch for the Lord and put it in the refrigerator with a note inside that says, 'I Love You.' "

To my surprise, Jane did just that. A few days later Jane told me what happened. As she made those lunches the first two days it was for the Lord, but by the third day she said that the lunch was made for her husband, Bill. She received a beautiful thank-you love note from her husband for a week of sack lunches. Surrender your ego to the needs of the other person.

2. *Pay attention to the other person.* Make your spouse feel special and unique, honoring and treating that person as you would want to be treated.

3. *See your man as your leader and hero.* You married him and saw his many fine qualities. Let's be willing to follow his leadership in spite of the fact that we may be smarter, stronger, greater, prettier, wiser, and even more organized. Over the years I've watched my Bob make mistakes that have cost us as a family. But today he has grown and learned from those areas. I can truly say I never said, "See, I told you so," even though I may have thought it. He already knew in his heart that he had made a mistake. I've been his helpmate, encourager, and supporter through those difficult times. I tell him what I think about the situation, then I must let him lead. Today he comes to me and seriously considers my input.

4. *Make your husband feel good about himself; build him up in his eyes, your eyes, and in the eyes of the world.* I have the opportunity to make my husband look and feel good. I love Bob's strong hands; he cares for them even though he works in the garden. I praise him for those clean, well-cared-for hands and his handsome silver hair. Building up our hero's masculinity and self-worth in his eyes and in the eyes of other people is so important.

5. *A smart woman will shower her man with love.* First Corinthians 13:4-8 (NASB) says, "Love is patient, love is kind, and is not jealous; love does not brag and is not arrogant, does not act unbecomingly; it does not seek its own, is not provoked, does not take into account a wrong suffered, does not rejoice in unrighteousness, but rejoices with the truth; bears all things, believes all things, hopes all things, endures all things. Love never fails."

Let's not waste time arguing day and night. A smart woman will love, love, love. It takes years to learn patience, to bite your tongue and overlook his faults. My Bob may not always be easy to love, but he is sure worth it. So who is the winner? We women are! We keep the harmony for us, for our children, and to preserve our love. We are the women who make or break the home. Proverbs 24:3,4 (NASB) says, "By wisdom a house is built, and by understanding it is established; and by knowledge the rooms are filled with all precious and pleasant riches."

The brokenness of our lives and homes can be repaired if we are willing. Jane was willing to pack a lunch for the Lord. Great women are willing to make positive changes, and those changes first come in our relationship with God.

Submit to Him—Give Him your family, yourself, and your failures. We will never change our mate or other people, but God can, He will, and He does.

Commit to Him—Give God your attitudes, your behavior, your stresses, your work, your career, and all the areas in which you feel the need for peace.

Receive or rededicate yourself to Christ. Be an active part of the family of God, and then wait and allow God to work in your family.

Remember the story of the three little pigs? If we build our spiritual lives out of straw, it is easy for the enemy (the big, bad wolf) to blow our homes down. He doesn't have to huff and puff too long before he has us just where he wants us. Well, you say, I read my Bible (sort of), I pray (occasionally), and I go to church (once in a while). It's like we've built our lives out of sticks—stronger than the straw, but still very weak. But when we build a strong foundation and have Jesus Christ as the cornerstone; make prayer a priority; read the Bible; attend church; have a teachable spirit; and grow and learn through workshops, seminars, and books, it's hard for that big, bad wolf to blow our brick homes down. We've built our homes on God's solid gold and silver.

Yes, we are liberated women:

- Liberated in our homes because we've built a strong foundation.
- Liberated in our lives as we live a life built with strong bricks.
- Liberated in our professions because we are creative women and can have a balance between home, work, family, and church.
- Liberated in traditionalism as we learn from the mistakes of the past and move toward the future with excitement and less stress.
- Liberated in Jesus Christ because He is our source of strength, love, forgiveness, peace, and joy.

4

How to Personally Feel Organized

*Always keep on praying.
No matter what happens, always be thankful,
for this is God's will for you
who belong to Christ Jesus.*

1 Thessalonians 5:17,18, TLB

❧ —— ❧

Do you ever look around your home, room, or office and just want to throw up your hands in disgust and say, "It's no use. I'll never get organized!" You need not feel that way anymore. With a few simple tools you can feel personally organized.

The old saying, "Everything has a place and everything is in its place," is a very helpful mind exercise. To help you accomplish this you need four tools:

- A "To Do" list
- A calendar
- A telephone/address source list
- A simple filing system

These four tools can drastically change your life from feeling confused to feeling organized. As you master these four organizational tools, you can branch out and acquire more skills, but these are the basis for a new beginning.

A "To Do" List

Have the first three of these tools be the same size ($8^1/_2$" x 11"; $8^1/_2$" x $5^1/_2$"; etc.). This way you won't have to fight with different sizes of paper. After arriving at your size of paper, write with a regular ink pen the words "To Do" at the top of the page, and begin writing down all the things that are in your head that you need to do. As you accomplish each item, you will get so much pleasure in crossing off what's been done. At the end of each day review your list and update any new things you need to add to your list. At the end of the week consolidate your several pages for the week and start again on Monday with a fresh page. As you get more experienced with this list, you will want to rank items by importance. The first is #1, the next is #2, and at the bottom of the page is #3. This added technique will help you maximize your time.

A Calendar

I personally recommend three types of calendars, the first being a two-page month-at-a-glance calendar. At one glance you get a good overview of the month. Details aren't written here, but you do jot down broad descriptions of engagements with times—for example, meetings, lunches, dinners, speaking engagements, dentist appointments, etc. The second type of calendar shows an entire week on a two-page format. *The Daily Planner* (Harvest House Publishers) also includes a small calendar for the month and room for notes on each week's section. The third type of calendar has a page for each day. On this day-at-a-glance calendar you get more detailed and specific and jot down what you will be doing for each hour or half hour. Be careful that you don't overload your calendar and jam your appointments too close together.

As a guideline I recommend that if you've been somewhere before and know where you're going, allow $1^1/_4$

times the amount of time you think the appointment will take. If you estimate that the meeting will last one hour, I block out one hour and 15 minutes on my calendar. If I've never been to where my appointment is, I allow 1½ times the amount of time I think it will take. If I estimate the meeting will last one hour, I block out one hour and 30 minutes on my calendar.

These three calendars will really make a big impact on your quest for organization.

A Telephone/Address Source List

This listing becomes your personal telephone and address book. In this book you design your own directory of information that you will use for home, work, or play. You might want to list certain numbers by broad headings such as: schools, attorneys, dentists, doctors, plumbers, carpenters, restaurants, etc. Broad headings help in looking up the specifics when you can't remember the person's last name.

If you have a client or customer listed, you might want to jot down personal data about the person so you can review before going to your next meeting. This information helps you identify with your customer. Certain items to jot down would be wife and children's names, sports of interest, favorite foods, favorite vacation spots, etc. The client will be impressed that you remembered all that information about him or her.

Use a pencil in writing down addresses and telephone numbers. It is much easier to correct them if people change either one.

A Simple Filing System

Our motto is "Don't pile it, file it." This principle will really tidy your area up. Go to your local stationery store and purchase about four dozen colored or 8½" x 14" manila file folders. I recommend colored file folders because they are brighter and add a little cheer to your day. I find that the legal size (8½″ x 14″) folders are more functional—they can accommodate the longer-sized papers.

On these folders, use simple headings for each: Sales Tax, Auto, Insurance, School Papers, Maps, Warranties, Taxes, Checks, etc. Then take all those loose papers you find around your home and put them in their proper place. Remember: "Don't pile it, file it." If you have a metal file drawer to house these folders, that's great. If not, just pick up a cardboard storage box to get started. Later you can move up to a better file cabinet.

Don't you already feel some relief by just reading about these four aids? It takes 21 consecutive days to acquire a new habit, so get on your mark, get set, GO!

5

Daily Scheduling

*She gets up before dawn to prepare
breakfast for her household, and plans
the day's work for her servant girls.*

Proverbs 31:15

❧ —— ❧

G od really did a number on me when I was
growing up because He prepared me for being
able to work with women today—to identify
with you, to know that you have these struggles in your
lives, and to help you be organized.

How do you take care of all these children and your
husband and still keep your priorities in order and glorify the Lord? It's difficult. There's no doubt about it.
We're going to talk about how we can do that—how we
can actually have more hours in our day. We're going to
work with what God tells us about how we can have
more hours in our day, and also how to be the type of
woman that God wants us to be.

The Night Worker

Let's start with our daily routine, and how we get
started daily in working these things out in our lives.
We're going to start with Proverbs 31:17,18, where God
tells us that the virtuous woman is energetic and a hard

worker, watches for bargains, and works far into the night. If we work far into the night, I guess that means we're going to have to start the night before in order to get ourselves together for the following day. Some of you are saying, "I've got a 24-hour job." You do, absolutely. If you have children at home, you are working 24 hours a day. Some of you were probably up three or four times last night with a sick baby. There's no doubt that God knows what He's talking about when He says you work far into the night, especially if you're a working woman. Your time is short at home, but being organized will help free you from guilt feelings about a messy home. We're going to start with the night before.

One of the ways in which you can do this is by gathering your laundry and sorting it out. A lot of these things you'll be able to teach your children to do. I encourage you to do that. My brother's children were with us for approximately four years. But during the time they were growing up, we wanted to give them as much responsibility as they could possibly handle at the youngest age they could handle it. This way they were not only working in our home as part of a family but also learning. By the time they got a little older we didn't have to teach them. We didn't have to worry, because they already knew how to do these things.

One of these things is gathering the wash the night before. Take a piece of fabric (a remnant or whatever—something with a lot of color in it) and make a laundry bag about 20 inches wide by 36 inches high. You might want to use a king-sized pillowcase with a shoelace strung through the top. Then say to your little ones, "Okay, we're going to play a game."

The Laundry Game

Don't tell them it's work. By the time they're ten, they will realize you've been working them to death, but they don't know it when they're little, so don't tell them. Say, "We're going to play a game, and it's called sort-the-laundry." Then get out your laundry bag that has lots of colors and say, "This is the bag where all the dirty clothes that have a lot of colors go. Now find something in this dirty-clothes pile that has a lot of colors." So they run over and pick it up, and you say, "Right! Now put it in the colored laundry bag." So they put it in there.

Then make a bag that is navy blue or dark brown and tell them, "This is where all the dark-colored clothes go." This would be the blue jeans, the brown T-shirts, the navy-blue socks—all those dark-colored clothes. "Now run over and find something that's dark-colored." You see, you're playing a game with them. They do it, and you say, "Great! That's absolutely right!" Then you make a bag that's all white, and you say, "Now this is where the white dirty clothes go—the white T-shirts, the white socks, the white underwear. They go into the white laundry bag."

Now you're going to give them a little test. You say, "Okay, now find me something that's colored." They run over and pick it up. And then, "Find something that's white." And they put it into the proper bag. What you're doing now is actually teaching children as young as four years old how to sort the laundry. When they're six and seven and ten, do you ever have to teach them again? No, because you've already taught them once.

Bags and More Bags

Another thing I did which really worked out well was to make individual laundry bags for each of the kids to hang in their room behind their door or in their closet. The three large laundry bags could go by your washing machine, in the garage, on the service porch, in the basement, or wherever you happen to have your laundry area. I made individual bags that were very colorful and matched the kids' rooms. This is where they put their own dirty clothes. Then whoever's job it was for the week to sort the laundry merely went around, collected everybody's laundry bag, and sorted these into the large laundry bags.

One gal gave me a great idea, which I think is fantastic if you have the room. Go out and buy three of those plastic trash cans in different colors, and put them in the garage. You can label them white clothes, dark clothes, and colored clothes with a felt-tip pen. Then your kids can sort the clothes by playing a basketball game with the clothes and trying to hit the right containers.

When summer comes and it's time for them to go off to camp, you can use the laundry bag as a duffel bag. You stick in their sleeping bag, their pillow, their hiking boots, and whatever. If any of you know what it looks like when they dump the sleeping bags into a pile at camp, there's this big pile of nothing but sleeping bags—they all look the same. The kids can't even remember their own name, let alone what their sleeping bag looks like, when they get off the camp bus. But our kids had lived with those laundry bags all year, so they knew what they looked like. They would pick out their laundry bag within a second, and they were relaxed and all set, ready for a week at camp. This way Mom solved a problem at camp even though she wasn't even there!

The Daily Work Planner Chart

Now take a good look at the Daily Work Planner Chart on page 47. What we would do, especially when we had the five children, was to take all the chores for the week, write them on individual pieces of paper, and put them in a basket. Then we would go around one by one and allow the children to choose—to pick out a chore. It was

❦ DAILY WORK PLANNER CHART ❦

Date __March 23-29__

	Mom	Dad	#1 Child	#2 Child	#3 Child	#4 Child	#5 Child
Saturday		— Clean out the garage — McDonalds — 6:00 P.M.					Feed dog
Sunday		Church — Family					↓
Monday	Laundry		Clean bedrm.			Fold clothes	Feed dog
Tuesday	Ironing	Set out trash	Rake leaves	Rake leaves	Rake leaves		
Wednesday	Housework		Vacuum house			Dust w/mom	
Thursday		Wash car		Help wash car			
Friday	Laundry	Set out trash	Mow lawn	Sweep walk-ways	Water plants		↓

like a little game; whatever they chose was the chore they had to do for the week. And it would go on the Daily Work Planner Chart.

They've chosen their own chore. They can't say, "Golly, how come I have to do this one again?" They chose it—it was their own fault. So they have to live with it for a week. Notice that Mom and Dad are listed on the chart too. What it shows the kids is that we're working together as a family. At the end of the day, when they've checked their charts and have done their chores as best they can, you can put a little happy face on the chart. Put on a Christmas tree if it's Christmas, or a little Easter cross if it's Easter. Stickers are great also. At the end of the week you can check your chart and say, "You know, our family did a fantastic job this week. We're going to have a picnic at the park (or go bicycling together, or have an evening with popcorn together, or do something else that's fun together) because we've really worked well together in accomplishing this." Do you see what that's doing? It's uniting your family.

Setting the Table

Another chore which can be delegated is setting the breakfast table the night before. A five-year-old can learn to set the table. It amazed me when our daughter, Jenny, would bring her friends home at 16 or 17 years of age and they didn't even know how to set a table. They didn't know where a knife, fork, and spoon went. It wasn't their fault. It was because Mom or Dad never took the time to teach them. As the five-year-old sets the table the night before you can say, "Okay, Timmy, do whatever you want. You can use Mom's good china, or you can use paper plates, or you can have candlelight, or you can put your favorite teddy bear on the table. I don't care—whatever you want to do."

Too many times we put the good china on the table only for when company comes and at Christmas. Who are the most important people in our lives? Our family! And we seldom use the good china for those people who mean the very most to us. I look at it this way: We can't take the china with us, so if a piece gets broken here and there, it gets broken. I would rather have my children be able to enjoy the nicer things and to use them and live with them than to have them in a china cabinet where they can't be enjoyed. So let your children have the freedom to use the good china and teach them as you go along how to set the table.

The Weekly Calendar

Now notice the Weekly Calendar on page 50. On this you can list those things which are going to go on for the week. Suzie has to be at the orthodontist, Timmy has football practice, and Bessie has Brownies. You can quickly look through the calendar and see when you're going to be needed, when you're going to need to pick up so and so. And you can feel free now because you know where you're needed and where your children will have to be. You check it over and fill it out the night before so you'll know what's happening the next day. Also fill in your work schedule if you work outside your home. Then your family can see it and know what's going on.

We women often have to get up early because, even though we have all the modern appliances, we still don't seem to have enough time. Why? Because we're not using our time effectively and efficiently. We have to get our homes organized, and for some of us that may mean getting up at five o'clock in the morning. If I were to ask you if you made your bed today, what would you answer? In our seminars about one-third of the women admit to not making their bed. How long does it take to make

❧ WEEKLY CALENDAR ❧

	Monday	Tuesday	Wednesday	Thursday	Friday	Saturday	Sunday
Morning							
Noon							
Night							

a bed? About two minutes—that's what the average woman says. So what's two minutes out of a whole day to make a bed?

I have a friend who never made her bed. She figured she would just get in it again at night, so why bother to make it? So she never made it. Now she has a son who is 20 years old and is an absolute slob. He's never made his bed because he never had an example. He doesn't know how to put a thing away. He doesn't even know that when he pulls out a drawer he should push it back in! Nothing is hung up, the bed is never made, and his room is an absolute disaster. It's not really his fault, though, because Mom never took the time to teach him to make his own bed and take care of his room.

The Bed Lesson

I asked our son after his second year in college, "Brad, do you make your bed at school?" He replied, "Mom, I'm the only one in my house who makes his bed." I know why he does it, because once when he was about eight years old he hadn't made his bed for four mornings in a row. I had let him get away with it a little now and then, but four mornings was just too much. He was halfway down the block with a couple of his little buddies when I noticed his unmade bed and went running after him. When I caught up with him I said, "Brad, I really hate to do this, but this is the fourth morning in a row you haven't made your bed. So I'm going to have to ask you to please go back in and make your bed." He replied, "Mom, you wouldn't!" I said, "Well, I'm really sorry, but I'm going to have to do it." He responded, "But I'm going to be late for school!" I came back with, "I know you're going to be late for school, but we'll worry about that later." So he came home and made his bed. Then he said, "You know I'm going to need a note for my teacher."

I replied, "Fine, I'll be happy to write you a note." I wrote him a note saying that Brad was late because this was the fourth morning in a row that he had not made his bed, and that the teacher could do whatever she wanted with him. You know what? I never had any trouble with Brad making his bed after that!

I'm not in a popularity contest to be the number-one mom, but I *am* striving to be the mom that God wants me to be. Now it was hard for me to do that to Brad. It was as hard for me to call him back into the house as it was for him to actually do it. But over the years it paid off, because it only happened one time. And after that he saw to it that his bed got made.

Also, let them learn to make their own bed. Don't go in and remake it. If you do, they will say, "Why should I even bother? Mom just remakes it anyway." Let them have crooked bedding. As time passes the bedding will become straighter and straighter.

Helping Them Come to Breakfast

After we make the bed we go into the kitchen. (We can get the first load of wash in beforehand if we like.) God tells us several times in the Bible that we can't be lazy women.

We get breakfast cooked and call everyone to the table for breakfast, but they don't come. Isn't that irritating? I think that was one of the things that bothered me the most. How are we going to correct this problem? I said to the children, "We're going to have a meeting." I continued, "You know, I've really got a problem. I call you children for breakfast, but you don't come. Now is there anything you might suggest that could help with this problem?" So they said to me, "Golly, Mom, if you'd just let us know a couple of minutes before breakfast is ready, we'd come right to the table." So that's what we did.

You can ring a chime, play the piano, sing a song, blow a whistle—whatever you want to do. Give them a warning to let them know that breakfast or dinner is going to be ready within a few minutes, and they'll come. It absolutely worked beautifully in our family.

Another thing—serve everyone at one time, and don't be a short-order cook. I may be a Christian today, but I'm still Jewish. I want to please everybody because I'm still that good little Jewish mother. So I was fixing French toast for Brad and omelets and pancakes for Jenny. I was fixing oatmeal or whatever they wanted. But what happened to me? I got exhausted. I thought, "This cannot go on." So that's when I came up with the Menu Planner.

The Weekly Menu Planner

I came up with some charts that I called the Weekly Menu Planner. I would have a different breakfast every day, but everyone would eat the same thing every morning. So when Brad came to the table and said, "Ick, I hate oatmeal," I replied to him, "Okay, so you don't like oatmeal. Tomorrow morning, as you see on the Menu Planner, we're going to have French toast, and that's your very favorite." So at least one morning a week we pleased at least one of the children. This worked so beautifully that I decided to extend the idea and make menus for the whole week. Sometimes I even went into two weeks. Also, I tried a new recipe at least once a week. (That adds a little variety.)

The Shopping List

I would make out my menus and then use my Shopping List. I would check off on the Shopping List everything I needed at the market that week in order to prepare the meals on the menu for that week. What

❦ WEEKLY MENUS ❦

Date **May 5**

	Breakfast	Lunch	Dinner
Monday	7 grain cereal	Sack lunch	Mexican mountains, salsa, dip
Tuesday	Pancakes w/ turkey patties		Baked chicken, baked potatoes
Wednesday	Scrambled eggs w/ wheat toast		Halibut w/ vegetables
Thursday	Belgian waffles w/ straw-berries		Stir fry w/ noodles
Friday	Oatmeal w/ rye toast		Italian pasta salad
Saturday	Eat out at Coco's	Turkey w/ cheese sandwiches	Bar-B-Q chicken, beans, biscuits
Sunday	Bran muffins, melons	meat loaf, potatoes, gravy	soup, salad, crackers

❦ SHOPPING LIST ❦

Date _May 5_

Qty.	Staples
_____	Cereal
_____	Flour
_____	Jello
_____	Mixes
_____	Nuts
_____	Stuffing
_____	Sugar

Spices
Qty.	
_____	Bacon Bits
_____	Baking Powder
_____	Chocolate
_____	Coconut
✓	Salt/Pepper
_____	Soda

Pasta
_____	Inst. Potato
_____	Mixes
✓	Pasta
_____	Rice
✓	Spaghetti

Drinks
✓	Apple Cider
_____	Coffee
✓	Juice
✓	Sparkling
_____	Tea

Canned Goods
_1_	Canned Fruit _Strawberry_
_____	
_____	
_____	Canned Meals
_____	Canned Meat
_____	Canned Vegetables
_____	
_1_	Soups _chicken_
_3_	Tuna

Condiments
Qty.	
_1_	Catsup
_____	Honey
_1_	Jelly/Jam
_____	Mayonnaise
_____	Molasses
_____	Mustard
_____	Oil
_1_	Peanut Butter
_____	Pickles
_____	Relish
_1_	Salad Dressing
_____	Shortening
_____	Syrup
_____	Tomato Paste
_____	Tomato Sauce
_____	Vinegar

Paper Goods
_____	Foil
_____	Napkins
_____	Paper Towels
_1_	Plastic Wrap
_____	Tissues
_____	Toilet Paper
_____	Toothpicks
_____	Trash Bags
_____	Waxed Paper
_____	Zip Bags
_____	Small
_1_	Large

Household
_____	Bleach
_____	Laundry Soap
_____	Dish Soap
_____	Dishwasher Soap
_1_	Fabric Softener
_____	Furniture Polish
_____	Light Bulbs
_____	Pet Food
_____	Vacuum Bags
_____	
_____	
_____	

Fresh Produce
Qty.	
_6_	Fruit _apple_
_6_	_oranges_
_4_	_banana_
_____	Vegetables
_1_	_celery_
_1_	_lettuce_

Personal Items
_____	Body Soap
_1_	Deodorant
_____	Fem. Protection
_____	Hair Care
_____	Makeup

Frozen Food
_____	Ice Cream
✓	Juice _orange_
✓	_pineapple_
_____	T.V. Dinners
_____	Vegetables
_____	

Pastry
_2_	Bread/s
_____	Buns
_____	Chips
_____	Cookies
_1_	Crackers
_____	Croutons

Meat
_____	Beef
_3_	Chicken
_____	

Dairy
_1_	Butter
_1 #_	Cheese
_1_	Cottage Cheese
_12_	Eggs
_1Q_	Milk
_____	Sour Cream
_____	

happens when you do this? You don't go to the market and buy things you don't need. You save yourself money, and you feel organized inside because you know you have your meals planned. You shop for them and have everything in the house that is going to be in those meals for the week.

Now, let's say Wednesday night comes and your husband calls you up and says, "Honey, I've had a terrible day. I don't even know if I can face anybody, but I want to be with you. Let's go somewhere, just you and me, for dinner." So you look at your Weekly Menu Planner and notice that you had meat loaf listed for that night. What do you do about that? You just move meat loaf over to the next week. Now you have everything in the house and one meal planned for next week. You give your kids waffles or hot dogs that night, and you go out with your husband and enjoy your time together. You can be very flexible with your menu planning, especially if you're a working woman. It's so wonderful to know that you have in your mind what needs to be fixed for that night. You almost get excited about going home from work to cook your dinner!

Do you realize that we make an average of 750 meals a year? It's a big area to be organized in. On my own Weekly Calendar, I would do my food shopping on Thursday, so I would always allow enough time on Thursday afternoon to take care of this. When I came home from the market I would then organize my food for all the rest of the week. If you've got several children, and particularly if they're hyperactive children, here is a great way to do it: As you come in from the market, you start delegating. One unloads the bags, one folds the bags, one puts away the frozen foods, one puts away the canned goods, and another puts away the dairy products and refrigerator foods. If you have a child who is a little older, you have him or her cleaning all the vegetables.

The Salad Solution

We're big salad and vegetable eaters in our house, so I would buy head lettuce, romaine lettuce, spinach, red leaf lettuce—all the different kinds of lettuce. I would dump them into the kitchen sink, fill it full of water, clean the lettuce carefully, and then set it aside to drain. But you know how it is—all the water never really gets out of the lettuce, so even if you put it in Tupperware or a baggie, the lettuce rusts. It won't last you as long as you need it to.

Here's how to solve your problem. In the variety section of the supermarket, or at a big drugstore, buy a lingerie bag. (It's a bag with a lot of holes in it.) Now take your lettuce leaves and put them into the lingerie bag. Then put the bag into the washing machine and turn on the machine at the spin cycle. This only takes 10-20 seconds. Then you take the lettuce back into the kitchen and tear it up into your Tupperware or baggie. Put it in the refrigerator, and it will last you one to two weeks.

Now what have you done? You've taken a few minutes to make a big tossed green salad. You never have to worry the rest of the week about making a salad. Now take all your vegetables and clean them and cut them up (your broccoli, zucchini, cauliflower, etc.). Put them in Tupperware or a baggie and store them in the refrigerator. Now everything is ready for steamed vegetables, if you have that on your menu for the week. All you have to do is take the vegetables out of the refrigerator and put them in your steamer, and you've got it all done. You'll save yourself hours throughout the week by investing that little bit of time.

I have another solution for you. Should you not want to go to the washing machine to put your lettuce in it, since you feel a little funny about that, buy yourself a tea towel and fold it in half. Sew it up on two sides, making a bag out of it, and attach a little bit of ribbon at the side. Now you have a lettuce bag. Put your lettuce in it, and the bag will absorb the water somewhat. Then put it into either your Tupperware or the lettuce compartment in your refrigerator, and you have a cute little lettuce bag. After 24 hours remove the lettuce bag, as it will be soaking wet. This method doesn't do the job as well as spinning the water out, but it still does a pretty good job. You can buy a plastic lettuce spinner at your local department store, but why spend more money when you already have a spinner in your laundry area?

Due to our busy schedules, the woman of the nineties needs all the help she can get when it comes to creative meal planning. Today's woman wants to feed her family high-fiber, low-fat, low-cholesterol diets. All of this and much, much more can be found in our cookbooks. Coauthor Sue Gregg and I have given you a realistic approach to a healthy lifestyle with three months of complete menu planning with all the high-fiber/low-fat and low-sodium recipes included. It's a great source of help for today's busy woman who wants to increase her family's nutrition. See page 343 for ordering instructions.

Back to Breakfast

At breakfast time ask each family member, "Where am I going to be needed today? Where do you need me?" Check your Weekly Calendar as you go over the day's plans with them.

Then have everyone take their dishes to the sink. We had a rule in our family that no one ever went to the kitchen empty-handed. Each person always had to pick something up and take it to the sink. I would fill up the sink with hot, sudsy water when I'd get in the kitchen in the morning, and then each person would put dishes into the hot, sudsy water, where they would stay for a little while until I was ready to get back to them. Now if you do this with your family, what happens? It's saving work for you. It's saving you steps so you have energy to do other things that are more important.

Then quickly check each child's room with him or her. Also quickly check the bathrooms, and have the children wipe the toothpaste off the mirror. Once or twice a week you might want to go in and do a really good job, but get them used to cleaning up after themselves so they won't think you're a little maid who will go around every day cleaning up after them. Then, as they're leaving the house, check to see if they have their lunch, their lunch money, their books, their homework, their gym clothes, their reports, or whatever they need.

Now we say farewell to our family, because it's time for the children and family to be getting off to school or work. We may even be going to work ourselves, so we really need to have things pulled together and organized. Proverbs 31:26 says, "When she speaks, her words are wise, and kindness is the rule for everything she says." What happens is that in the morning when things are hassled and we're moving around quickly because we've got to get the children ready for school, we can become very irritated. Also, we had to make the bed this morning, and we're not really used to doing that. But at this point we say to our husband, "Honey, is there anything I can do for you today? Is there anything you need me to do for you today?" Maybe you need to go to the hardware store for him. He'll fall over in a dead faint the first morning you ask him, but then he will probably come up with a nice list of errands the next day.

One thing that bothered me a lot was that just when I really got into my housework the phone would ring and one of the kids would say, "Oh, I forgot such-and-such. Would you bring it to school?" So you drive to their school and you look all over campus for your child who forgot something. And you've lost an hour of your day before you know it. So take those few minutes to check with the kids in the morning, before they leave the house, to see that they have everything they need.

Say Something Good

When your kids have done something well, be sure to compliment them on it. I teach a Friday morning Bible study in my home, and one day I thought I would throw out this suggestion to the women: "Write down six items that you like about yourself." You wouldn't believe how hard this was for them. They were hemming and hawing around. They couldn't figure out anything to write down. You see, what happens over the years is that we've had parents, plus brothers and sisters, plus teachers who have repeatedly put us down. So as we've grown up we've developed bad self-esteem.

Therefore we need to compliment our children when they do something well. "Timmy, you did such a neat job setting the table this morning. I just love the way you put your teddy bear on the table." You know what's going to happen tomorrow morning? He won't be able to wait to show what else he's done for you, and he'll become eager to do these chores. "Susie, I'm so pleased with you today—you got your shoes on the right feet, and your socks match. Thank you so much for working on that." As you begin to compliment them and build into them a good self-esteem, and as you send them off with a loving hug, you help them to remember you as a smiling mother and not as a screaming shrew.

God says in Proverbs 31:17 that the virtuous woman is energetic and a hard worker. So we gals can't fall back into bed, can we? Besides, the bed is made, so it's not quite so tempting to get back into it! We have to keep going, to get the second load of wash in, to get the dishes done. Now we can check our Menu Planner to see what we're going to have for dinner tonight, to see that we've taken what we need out of the freezer. Remember, we have all those things in the house already, so we feel free and comfortable about our meals for the day. Then we get our counters cleaned up and water our houseplants, and we rejoice that our basic housework is done at only 9:00 in the morning. For you women who work outside your home, it could be 7:00 A.M., and for you moms of preschoolers it might be 1:00 P.M.

The Right Priorities

God tells us in Proverbs 31:27-29, "She watches carefully all that goes on through out her household, and is never lazy. Her children stand and bless her; so does her husband. He praises her with these words: 'There are many fine women in the world, but you are the best of them all!'"

How do we receive that kind of praise from our children and our husband? There's only one way that I know of that will cause them to give us that genuine kind of praise, and that's by having our priorities as a Christian woman in order.

Do you know what our priorities are? God tells us in Matthew 6:33 (KJV), "Seek ye first the kingdom of God and his righteousness; and all these things shall be added unto you." Our number-one priority is God. There have been times in my life when I got my priorities out of order. There was a time when I needed to have a special time with my Lord, but the only time available was at 5:00 in the morning, when the house was still. And that was hard, because I might have been up three times during the night with the children. But I got up and spent that little bit of time. I committed my works to the Lord, and my plans were established (Proverbs 16:3).

On some days, I would check my calendar and say, "There's no way I'm going to get everything done that I have to do today." But then I would get up early in the morning, read a little in God's Word, put my hands on the calendar, and say, "Lord, You know what I have to do today. Would You help me and guide me through every moment of the day? Show me what You will have me to do." Do you know what happened on the days I did that? I got everything done and had time for a nap in the afternoon.

The Other Priorities

Our second priority is our husband. Our third priority is our children. Our fourth priority is our home. And number five is all the other things. That means helping a philanthropic group, being a Brownie leader, leading a Bible study, having luncheons out with the ladies, shopping, and all those things. I'll never forget the day my husband came to me and said, "Emilie, you love those children more than you do me." Well, I had to take care of the children. I said, "They need me. I have to do all these things for them." But in my heart I knew he was right. I knew he was being neglected because he was telling me he didn't feel that he had priority in my life over the children.

We women often get our priorities mixed up. I still struggle with it. Sometimes the number-one priority, which is God, becomes number six or seven on the list. Husband can be number eight or nine. Children can be number one, and all the other things we do number two. We're good at that. But God tells us that our children will stand and bless us, and so will our husbands, as long as we get our priorities in order. So remember that God is there. He's given those children to you as a gift. He's going to take care of them for you. Keep them in the right priority. Remember that you were a wife to your husband before you were a mother to your children.

Someday, and it won't be long, those children are going to be out of the nest. They're going to be creating homes and families of their own and will be going off to college and work. And then you and your husband will be alone in that home. If you haven't worked on developing a relationship and spending time together and making him an important priority in your life, at that point you'll look at each other and either love and know and communicate with each other, or else simply be two strangers. Great marriages just don't happen, but are grown through much care.

If you're working outside the home and have your priorities out of order, I recommend to you that you stop working until you get those priorities in order. You say, "But I have to work." I had a woman come up to me after a class and say, "Boy, I didn't like what you said. I was working and I loved my job." (Her husband was an unbeliever, and she was having trouble in her marriage.) She continued, "That job was so important to me, but my house was all out of order. That's why I came to the organization class. I just rejected everything you said. After two weeks, things got even worse in my home, and I began thinking. God began to work in my heart. He said, 'You'd better get your home in order.' So I decided that I was going to quit my job and work on my priorities and get my home organized and in order. So I went to my husband and said to him, 'Honey, I'm going to quit my job.' He replied, 'Who's going to pay the car payment?' I said, 'Sell the car.' He responded, 'Well, okay.' So I quit my job."

Later she said to me, "I got my home in order. I got all the things done that I needed to do. Now my relationship with my husband is getting better. Soon we're going to have a Valentine party at our church."

She continued, "He had never before set a foot into our church, but I thought I would invite him one more time. I said, 'We're having a Valentine dinner at church; would you like to go with me?' He replied, 'Yes, I would.' If I had planned that evening myself, it couldn't have been better. Later my husband said to me, 'Let me know anytime you have something at church that's special. I'd like to go with you.' "

So you see, when you get your priorities in order, God will take care of the rest. Today that husband is a growing Christian.

Evening Time

It's evening time. We can get a fire lit and some candles going. We may prepare a few little munchies. (Remember, we've got everything all prepared. All the vegetables are cut and cleaned in the refrigerator.) We can make a dip with a little sour cream, cottage cheese, garlic salt, and lemon juice. If the kids get a little wild, we can just throw a sheet on the floor, give them some veggies and a little dip, and let them have a little fun.

You know, the five o'clock hour can be a terrible time. The children are tired of you and you are certainly tired of them by then. So you may need to prepare yourself a bit. Freshen up your makeup. (Remember, it was six o'clock in the morning when you first put your makeup on.) Put on a little perfume. And then start thinking toward a quiet and gentle spirit. How can you possibly do that? Well, God tells us that we are to start thinking of a quiet and gentle spirit.

But right now it's five o'clock and a zoo around the house. There's spilled milk all over the kitchen floor, and something's boiling over on the stove. The dog and cat are hungry and nipping at your heels. You've got kids all around you. Then the phone rings. And you're supposed to have a quiet and gentle spirit? It's tough, isn't it? Do you know what I did? I would go into the bathroom and stick my head in the sink and pray several times, "Lord, You don't know what it's like out there. It's a war zone." I'd cry. Sometimes I'd have to make three or four trips in and out of the bathroom until I would finally pull myself together enough to settle down the children and reorganize as best I could.

Hopefully I would be ready for my husband's arrival. When I heard his car coming up the driveway, or him walking up the driveway, I would drop everything and go to greet him. Now I know you may be diapering that baby, but throw a diaper over him and go and greet your husband. What does it tell him when you run to the door to greet him as he comes in from work? You're telling him that he's important to you. He's number one. You don't know how long he's been on the freeway. You don't know what happened at work today—whether he had to fire his best friend, or whether the construction job fell through. You do not know what went on that whole day.

That husband of yours could have gone a hundred different places that night. There are tons of women out there who would like your husband. I don't care what he looks like or what kind of shape he's in. They'd like him. But he has chosen to come home to you. He's coming through that door to you, so take those few minutes. Go to the door, greet him, throw your arms around him. Tell him that you're happy he's home, that you're thankful he's worked hard all day and provided for this home, for you and your children. Then let him have a few minutes to unwind with the newspaper, mail, or children. Try not to share the negative parts of the day with him until after dinner.

Then enjoy your family. God has given that family to you as a gift. If we're raising little wild Indians, they're not fun to enjoy, are they? Maybe only Mom and Dad can put up with them. But other people don't want to be around them. So lovingly discipline them. Teach them obedience and responsibility. They're a very precious legacy that God has given to you. They grow up very quickly, and they will grow up to be beautiful children if you lovingly discipline them.

On the following pages you will find examples of charts to help organize your daily life.

The Family Household Expenditures Chart

Ecclesiastes 3:1 (NIV) says, "There is a time for everything, and a season for every activity under heaven"—and that means even for organization. On the Family Household Expenditures Chart, each month you can list your expenses for your house payment or rent, food, utilities, babysitting, insurance, telephone, clothing, beauty parlor, taxes, and donations. Then at the end of the year you'll have the totals for all the expenses you've had during the year, and this will be very easy to take to your tax person.

The Family History Chart

The next section is your Family History Chart. Here you can list your children's names, their birth dates, their blood types, dates of their yearly physical, their dental exams, their eye exams, when they had their inoculations, etc. Everything is nicely listed here so you can refer back to it.

Shopping Guide Chart

The family Shopping Guide Chart is a practical way of knowing how your family grows. This will enable you to quickly give grandparents and family children's clothing sizes and also can be used for medical growth questions and patterns. It will also be an interesting chart to see the growth patterns of children in future years.

The Credit Cards Sheet

The next section is your Credit Cards Sheet. You should list the name of the company, the account number, the address, the telephone number, and when the card expires. Then, if it's lost or stolen, you can quickly go to your notebook and report it immediately. If you do some purchasing over the telephone, you have the number handy, and you won't have to fumble through your purse trying to find your credit card.

The Important Numbers Sheet

Then there's the Important Numbers Sheet. List phone numbers for the police, the fire department, the ambulance service, the poison control service, the neighbors, etc.

One woman said to me, "I started making out my notebook when I came to this Important Numbers Sheet. I started listing all the telephone numbers. Then I noticed the Poison Control heading. Well, I hadn't even known that there was such a thing! So I looked through the phone book, but I couldn't find the number. I called the information operator, but she didn't know too much about it either. It took me several minutes to finally get the number of the poison control. That listing on the chart could have saved a child's life. If my child had taken something and I had to try to find the number, it could have been four or five minutes before I could have found it."

Dates and Occasions

Then you have a list of Dates and Occasions. List everybody's birthday, everybody's anniversary, and all the other important dates for the year. As each month comes up, check to see whose birthday is listed. You can show on the chart if you sent a card or what kind of gift you gave last year.

The Home Instructions Sheet

A Home Instructions Sheet comes next. If you should go away on vacation, or someone should come into your home to take care of your children, they can see what time Sunday school starts, where the church is, any appointments you may have during the week, and when the trash is picked up. Maybe your mother-in-law sees this man walking around in your backyard one day, and she doesn't know who he is. She can check the Home Instructions Sheet and say, "That's the pool man, or that's the gardener, so I'm not going to worry about him."

The Entertainment Sheet

Then there's an Entertainment Sheet. This is excellent because if you're going to have a party or a buffet, you can list the guests, the time and date, what type of party, if you're going to have a theme, your menu, your table decorations, etc. You can also write down any notes that you might want to make after the evening is over.

Tips on Taxes

Purchase a dozen 5" x 10" envelopes. These are for all your receipts and check stubs, one for each month of the year. Insert all your receipts and check stubs in the envelopes. Then take these envelopes plus your expenditures sheet to your tax preparer and everything is in order to make out your return.

These charts—plus the Weekly Calendar, Menu Planner, Grocery List, and Work Planner charts—come professionally bound in an 8½" x 11" three-ring notebook with a one-year supply. (See page 343 for ordering information.)

FAMILY HOUSEHOLD EXPENDITURES
Month of January

House Payment/Rent	Food	Utilities	Furniture/Repairs	Car/Gas	Insurance	Phone	Clothing	Cleaning: House, Clothing	Haircuts	School Expenses
929.00	72.13	102.40	car 76.02	21.00	427.00 car	72.00	15.00	14.00	25.00	5.00
	50.76			17.50	170.00 med.	23.00	41.00	45.00	7.00	4.00
	39.00			18.00			16.00		4.50	3.75
	83.40			20.00			30.00		5.00	6.04
	24.24									
	62.43									
929.00										
Totals 331.96	102.40	76.02	76.50	597.00	95.00	102.00	59.00	41.50	18.79	

🦢 DEDUCTIBLE ITEMS 🦢

Credit Card Charges	Investments	Medical/ Dental	Medicines	Babysitting	Taxes	Donations	Savings	Other Misc. Expenses
47.00 B/A	60.00 mutual fund	25.00	18.00	—	225.00	175.00	100.00	60.00 United Way
								10.00 Booster Club
								10.00 Boy Scouts
47.00								
Totals	60.00	25.00	18.00		225.00	175.00	100.00	80.00

❧ FAMILY HISTORY ❧

Family Member Name	Birth Date	Blood Type	Date of Last: Yearly Physical	Date of Last: Dental Exam	Date of Last: Eye Exam	Innoculation/ Date	Other
Christine	7/9/83	B	12/83	7/84	—	at 18 mo.	
			12/84	1/85	—	DPT	
			12/85	6/85	—	Rubella	
				12/85	12/85	Measles	
Chad	11/29/84	B	12/15/85	—	—	6 mo.-DPT	
						Polio 5/85	

❧ SHOPPING GUIDE ❧

| Family Member Name | Sizes | | | | | Favorite Activities | Other Clubs, Interests, Etc. |
	Dress/Suit	Shoes	Pants	Socks	Underwear		
Dad	46 R	10½ D	38 x 30	11-13	XL	Gardening	Reading
Mom	6	8	6	8	6	Cooking	Walking
Brad	42 R	10 D	32 x 30	11-13	M	Biking	Running
Jennifer	7/8	7½	7	7/9½	M	Aerobics	Decorating
Christine	8	3	8	10-12	S	Dancing	Singing
Chad	7	2	6		S	Baseball	Swimming
Bevan	7	12	6	6/7	S	Legos	Baseball

❦ CREDIT CARDS ❦

If lost or stolen, notify company at once

Company	Card Number	Company Address	Company Phone Number	Card Expires (Date)
Bank of America		7264 Orchibald St. San Francisco, Ca. 94100	555-8421	
Shell Oil		1123 Sage Brush Phoenix, Az. 85012	555-3321	
American Express		62431 Hilltop Ln. Boston, Ma. 02106	555-4306	
Diner's Club		2731 Hale Ave. Los Angeles, Ca. 90001	555-6626	

❦ IMPORTANT NUMBERS ❦

Service Person	Phone Number	Service Person	Phone Number
Ambulance	555-4203	Neighbor - Sally	555-0011
Appliance Repair	555-4219	Newspaper	555-4738
Dentist - Merrihew	555-4203	Orthodontist	555-1104
Doctor - Turnbull	555-4909	Pastor	555-0767
Electrician - Rusty	555-1001	Poison Control	555-0013
Fire	555-9996	Police	555-5001
Gardener - Mike	555-4618	Pool Service	—
Gas Co. Emergency	555-5551	Plumber	555-0114
Glass Repair		School(s) - Elem.	555-9013
Heating/Air Conditioning Repair Person	555-0013	School(s) - Jr. High	555-1111
Husband's Work	555-0321	Veterinarian	—
Insurance (Car)	555-0112	Cat's Name	Tiger
Insurance (Home)	555-0112	Dog's Name	Mickie
		Animal Control	555-0014
		Security system	555-1163
		Trash	555-0731
		newspaper boy	555-4100

❦ DATES AND OCCASIONS ❦

Month	Date/Occasion	Name of Person(s)	Gift(s) Given
January	Jan. 10	Don Foor graduation	Dress shirt
February	Feb 13	Bill Beck promotion	Necktie
March	Mar. 22	Yoli Brogger graduation	Sport dress
April	Apr. 11	Craig's birthday	Sport shirt
May	May 22	Brad's birthday	Jogging shoes
June	June 8	Bob's birthday	3 days in San Diego
		Bill's birthday	swim trunks
	June 9	Ken's birthday	walk shorts

DATES AND OCCASIONS (continued)

Month	Date/Occasion	Name of Person(s)	Gift(s) Given
July	July 9	Christine's birthday	$50.00 Bond
August	Aug. 8	Great Grandma Gertie's 80th birthday	A cruise to Alaska
September	Sept. 30	Bob & Emilie's 39th anniversary	A cruise to Mexico
October			
November	Nov. 18 Nov. 20	Jenny's birthday Chad's birthday	Gift certificate $50.00 Bond
December	Dec. 13 Dec. 10	Bevan's birthday Bradley Joe	Winter coat

🐛 HOME INSTRUCTIONS 🐛

	Routine Chores/Errands	Special Appointments
Sunday	Christine & Chad's Sunday school begins 9:45	Grandparents to take home after church
Monday	Water front plants Feed bird Bring in paper each morning	Chad's Dentist appointment 2:30
Tuesday	Set out trash	
Wednesday	Water front lawn Feed bird	mail off letters, bills
Thursday	Gardener comes today	
Friday	Set out trash Feed bird	
Saturday	Water indoor plants	

❦ ENTERTAINMENT ❦

Date January

Guests	Time/Date		Dinner/Party Type	Menu	Decorations/Centerpiece/Tablecloth
Delorenzos	1/8	6:30 P.M.	Beans & cornbread	Beans, corn-bread, salad	Farm Animals
Menitews	1/15	7:00 P.M.	Pasta & salad	Pasta, salad, garlic bread	Dripping candles in old wine bottles
Blanchons	1/22	6:00 P.M.	mexican	Tacos, Chicken fajitas, enchiladas	Sombrero, gorda
Handricksons	1/29	6:30 P.M.	French	veal, sauces, potatoes	Candlelight w/dinner music

ENTERTAINMENT (continued)

Games/Entertainment	Dress	Help: Hired/Voluntary	Notes
Cards	Casual	—	A great time
Monopoly	Casual	—	We want them back
Charades	mexican	—	Fun, Fun, Fun
no structure	Casual	—	We will be with them in march

6

Stop Wasting Motions

The Lord is not slow in keeping his promise,
as some understand slowness.
He is patient with you,
not wanting anyone to perish,
but everyone to come to repentance.

2 Peter 3:9, NIV

❧ —— ❧

On our Volkswagen van we have a colorful rainbow with "More Hours in My Day" lettered on the side. We have a lot of people from the service station attendant to the nurseryman comment, "How do you get more hours in your day?" Everyone is looking for that little white pill that gives them that magic commodity called *time*.

I really can't give you one simple trick that makes it all flow together; however, I've found that if you can eliminate long searches for whatever you're looking for it will help you save time.

Group Your Shopping Trips Together

In your organizational notebook keep a list of items you need to buy: books, videos, Christmas gifts, clothes, cosmetics, housewares, birthday and anniversary gifts. When you see a sale or go to an outlet store, you can acquire what's on your list. This will save time and a lot of money later.

Purchase More Than One Like Item

If you have frequent demands for items like toiletries, pens, rulers, tape, and scissors, store several of each in strategic spots around the house. Don't waste time running all over the house to obtain a basic item. I especially did this when we had a two-story home. An extra vacuum cleaner and cleaning items were great for the upstairs.

Plan on Doing More Than One Thing at a Time

Most women can do more than one thing at a time very easily with a little training. I find that a long phone extension cord in my kitchen is a must. I can do any number of things while talking to a friend or relative. I also have a "to read" folder that I take with me when I know I'm going to have to wait. I get caught up with all my junk mail (if I even keep it), letters, correspondence, etc. I even carry along a few thank-you notes so I can write a friend. If you're into exercise and you have an indoor exercise machine this is a great time to read your favorite book as you work out on your treadmill.

Cut Unwanted Calls Short

Cut unwanted calls short by learning how to handle these graciously. These types of calls can really eat up valuable time.

Determine What's Important

This is where my "To Do" list really comes in handy. Each evening before going to bed or before leaving the office I make a list of what I need to do tomorrow, then I go one step further. I rank items according to priority: one, two, three, etc. Tomorrow morning I start working with number one, then go to number two. It's not long before I've made a real impact on that list.

Use Your Body Clock

Each of us operates most efficiently at a certain time of day. Schedule taxing chores for the hours when your mind is sharpest. Do these chores when you have the most energy.

Prevent Interruptions

In a recent article I read that most people are interrupted at least once every five minutes. If this is true for you, then analyze what's causing those interruptions. You are unique and will have unique situations. Our family always wanted to know "What's for breakfast or dinner?" so I posted the menu on the refrigerator door and it stopped these interruptions.

Store Your Keys and Glasses in One Area

My Bob used to always waste time looking for the car keys and his glasses. One day I put up a decorative key hook by the phone in the kitchen and told him to put his car keys on the hook and to place his glasses on the counter underneath the keys. Done deal—no more problem.

Plastic Clothes Bins for School Homework

Reduce that early-morning stress looking for the children's homework and school-related materials. If you are into color-coding your children's belongings, purchase colored plastic clothes bins and put them by the door from which the children leave each day for school. All they have to do is go to that door and reach down and gather their school supplies.

Have It Picked Up and Delivered

We're returning back to the good old days. More and more companies are offering these services. They are a valuable time-saver, and in many situations they are cost-efficient.

Start Using a Daily Planner

In this way you can stop looking for your keys, checkbook, list of appointments, address book, etc. They are all in your daily notebook. There are even stylish organizers which become a purse and housing for your planner. This two-in-one organizer really helps consolidate these two areas of your life.

Divide Big Jobs into Instant Tasks

In many of my books I talk about breaking the whole into smaller parts which become "instant tasks." These are little tasks you can handle. It's the big items that throw you.

Become a List Maker

In my daily planner I have a list for almost everything I do—all the way from planning a tea for a group of friends to planning a Christmas party. I save these notes so next time I can go back and review my comments. It's a great way to start planning since you already have a good beginning.

Plan Your Errands

Do the whole group at one time. My Bob is the greatest at this. I'm continually amazed at how much he gets accomplished when he leaves to run errands. He has his list in hand, with the order of his stops. Within a short time he's back and I'm overwhelmed.

Stop Procrastinating

That's why I like my "To Do" list. It helps me get started. Start the engine and get in motion. Even if all your ducks aren't lined up, get moving. A car has to be moving in order for it to go somewhere. *Start now!*

It Doesn't Have to Be Perfect

This goes hand in hand with procrastination—not wanting to do something if it's not perfect. It's nice to want things done right, but not if you are crippled into inactivity. You may know the difference, but your friends and guests won't know it's not perfect. Some jobs don't need perfection. Just do it.

Become a person who takes control of your time—don't let time control you. With a little study you can turn those negative "time-interrupters" into positive "time-savers."

7

Purse Organization

*I know it is not within the power
of man to map his life and plan
his course—so you correct me, Lord;
but please be gentle.*

Jeremiah 10:23,24

ந —— ந

Pete has just returned with the babysitter and you're running late for that long-looked-forward-to class reunion. But you want everything to be perfect.

Julie has spilled the cat's milk dish and you're sticking to the kitchen floor, trying to clean up the milk. The phone rings and the rollers are falling out of your hair. "Time—I need more time!" You're crying. Pete takes over the mess. Your sitter holds baby Jason, and you put Julie in her rocker with a book. Now it's time for you. You're hurrying to get ready and be out of the house on time. Grabbing your cute clutch pocketbook that matches your outfit, you begin to change purses. As you try to decide what to take out of your everyday bag with papers, gum wrappers, pacifiers, etc., rolling around the bottom, you begin to get upset and frustrated. Dumping the whole contents of the purse on the bed, you throw up your hands and say, "Forget it!" You may even end up taking your crummy tote bag that doesn't match or coordinate at all with your lovely outfit.

However, if you keep a well-organized purse, it will be so simple to change bags and do it quickly. You will never need to hassle with purse-changing again.

Getting Started

What you'll need is a nice-sized purse for everyday use. Choose a purse size to fit your frame—not too small and not too large. Then you'll need three to seven little purses. They can be made of quilted fabric (with zipper or Velcro fasteners) or of denim or corduroy prints (make each little purse different in color and size to identify it more easily). These little bags can also be purchased. Your everyday handbag should be pretty good-sized, since it's the one you'll be dragging around with you (and your kids) in and out of the market and all over the place. It should have everything in it that you'll need. Practically your whole life is now in your handbag.

The Wallet

First, you'll need to find a wallet that's functional for you. A wallet is very, very important. You want a wallet that has a little section where you can keep a few bills. Then it should have a zipper compartment where you can keep some change. (You should also keep a pen with your wallet.) Keep your most frequently used credit cards, your checkbook, your driver's license, and all those other little important things in your wallet. So now when you run to the cleaner or the pharmacy to pick something up, rather than taking your big purse with everything in it, all you have to do is pull your wallet out of your purse, run in, and make your little exchange. Then you put the wallet back into your purse.

The Little Bags

In the little bags you'll keep all sorts of things. One bag holds my sunglasses. In my makeup bag I keep such things as a mirror, lipstick, lipliner, lipgloss, spot remover, perfume, blush, nail clippers, nail file, etc. I also keep some change for an emergency phone call.

In addition to my wallet, sunglasses bag, and makeup bag, I keep in my purse a bag for reading glasses, and two more small bags for various items.

Everything Organized

Remember the day that Sue called you and said she wanted to go out to lunch with you? Well, now if you decide to go to lunch, you just grab your clutch purse and put a few of the little bags in it. For example, you'll want to take your wallet and credit cards plus your makeup bags. How long will this take you? Not even a minute. You just stick your purse under your arm, and you're off for the day. And when you come home again, you just take out the little bags and put them back into your everyday purse.

Items for Your Purse

A. Wallet:

pen/checkbook	driver's license
change compartment	calendar (current)
money/credit cards	pictures (most used)

B. Makeup Bag 1:

lipstick	mirror
comb/small brush	telephone change
blush	

C. Makeup Bag 2:

nail file	scissors (small)
small perfume	Kleenex tissues
hand cream	breath mints/gum/
nail clippers	cough drops
matches	

D. Eyeglass case for sunglasses

E. Eyeglass case for reading/spare glasses

F. Small Bag—Etc. Bag 1:
   business cards (yours and your husband's) for:
   —hairdresser
   —insurance person
   —auto club
   —doctor (health plan)
   library card
   seldom-used credit cards
   small calculator
   tea bag/Sweet 'n' Low/aspirin

G. Small Bag—Etc. Bag 2:
   reading materials—small Bible/paperback book
   toothbrush
   Wash 'n' Dry
   needle/thread/pins/thimble
   Band-Aid
   toothpicks
   collapsible cup
   Basic H cleaner
   tape measure
   feminine protection

8

Wardrobe Organization

*Fix your thoughts on what is true
and good and right . . . and dwell on the
fine, good things in others.*

Philippians 4:8

     🙙 —— 🙙

N ow let's get into our closet and get organized.
Let's weed out some of those things we don't
need and get our closets in order.

The Right Equipment

As we get into our wardrobe, we'll need some equipment with which to get organized. First we'll need some boxes with lids. Then we'll need some materials to cover shoeboxes. (Shoes that you don't wear often can go in shoeboxes covered with leftover wallpaper and labeled with a felt-tip pen. This way you'll have a nice-looking closet instead of just having funny-looking shoeboxes lying around.)

Then you may want to get some clear plastic boxes. In these you can put your scarves and belts and little clutch bags. Then get some plastic hangers. Get rid of those wire hangers that are always getting tangled together and get instead some cute plastic hangers in different colors. (You may want to color-coordinate your wardrobe.) A great way to save space is to get a slack rack. You can hang up to five pairs of pants on one of these, and it will take up the space of just one pair of pants in your closet. These are also wonderful to hang tablecloths on. (As you make tablecloths out of your sheets, just hang them on a slack rack.)

You'll also need some storage boxes for the clothes that you really want to keep but are not using right now.

Getting Started

How do we get started? We get three trash bags and label them "Put Away," "Give Away," and "Throw Away." As we walk into each closet we take everything out.

As you pull those things out of your closet, keep in mind that if you haven't worn it for the past year it goes in one of those three bags. Either you're going to put it away somewhere else, or you're going to give it away to somebody else, or you're going to throw it away. If you haven't worn it for two or three years, you'll definitely have to give it away or throw it away.

Taking Inventory

Now let's start taking inventory. (You can use the Wardrobe Inventory sheet printed in this chapter.) As you begin to take your inventory, you'll quickly begin to see what you have and need. For example, you may have way too many pairs of navy-blue pants. You only need one pair of good navy-blue pants and maybe a couple pairs of nice jeans. You can begin to see where you've made your mistakes as you take your wardrobe inventory, and you'll be able to start correcting those mistakes.

Everything in Its Place

Hang your things up as you put them back into your closet. Each thing should have a definite place. For example, all the extra hangers can go at the left end of your closet. Then arrange all your blouses according to color, then your pants, then your skirts, etc. If you have a jacket that matches your pants, separate them. (Hang the jacket with the jackets and the pants with the pants.) This way you can mix or match your things and not always wear the same jacket and pants together.

Your shoes can go on shoe racks. Some neat different kinds of shoe racks are now available, or you can cover shoeboxes with wallpaper or Christmas paper. (Your children can help you do this.)

Your smaller handbags can go in clear plastic boxes. The larger ones can go up on the shelf above your wardrobe. A hanging plastic shoe bag is great because you can also put your purses and scarves in it. Belts and ties should go on hooks. Ribbons can be hung on these hooks, too. Or you can just hammer a big nail into the wall. You'd be surprised at how many belts you can get on a nail!

Boxes Again

Be sure to number your storage boxes. If you're using file cards, number each card to correspond with the number of the box holding your extra clothing. Then list on the card what you have in the box.

WARDROBE ORGANIZATION SUMMARY

Equipment Needed
- Three to ten large storage boxes with lids
- Three large trash bags
- Materials to cover shoeboxes, such as wallpaper, contact paper, or even fabric to match bedroom colors
- Clear plastic boxes for scarves and clutch handbags

- Plastic hangers, all one color if you like
- Two to four hooks
- Belt or tie holder

How to Get Started

A. Label trash bags:
   1. Put Away
   2. Throw Away
   3. Give Away

B. Plan a one- to two-hour time (or several days of a shorter block of time) and think toward an orderly closet.
   1. Take everything out.
   2. Get vicious and make decisions.
   3. Put items in proper boxes. The rule to guide you is: If you haven't worn it for one year, it must be put away somewhere else or given away; if for two years, it doesn't belong in the closet; and if for three years or longer, give it away or throw it away. (There might be a very few exceptions.)
   4. Use your Wardrobe Inventory sheet.
      a. Return items to your closet and list them on your Wardrobe Inventory sheet.
      b. Suggested order for your clothes:
         1) Extra hangers
         2) Blouses
         3) Pants
         4) Skirts
         5) Blazers and jackets
         6) Sweaters (these can also be folded and put on a shelf or in a drawer)
         7) Dresses
         8) Gowns
      c. For each item, put all similar colors together (example: light to dark).

d. Coats and heavy jackets can be kept in a hall closet or in an extra wardrobe closet.

e. Shoes:
   1) Shoe racks—floor type or hanging
   2) Covered shoeboxes can be put on shelf or neatly stacked on floor.

f. Handbags:
   1) Smaller ones in clear plastic boxes
   2) Larger ones on shelf above wardrobe
   3) A hanging plastic shoe bag is also great for your handbags. It can be purchased in the notions section at any department store.

g. Belts and ties:
   1) Belt rack applied to wall with screws
   2) Hooks are great and easy to use and attach

Notes About Hangers

A. Wire hangers are messy and they crease clothing. Toss and replace them as you can with plastic or cloth-covered hangers.

B. Hang skirts on proper skirt hangers with clothespin-type clips.

C. Pants can be hung on a skirt hanger or folded in half over a plastic pant hanger.

Storage—Put Away Boxes

A. Get boxes with lids and number each box.

B. Assign each box a 3″ x 5″ card with a corresponding number. For example:

Box 1— Jenny's summer shorts, T-shirts, skirts, sandals

Box 2— Costume clothing: 1950s outfit, black-and-white saddle shoes, purple angora sweater with holes, high school cheerleader's outfit

Box 3— Ski clothes, socks, underwear, sweaters, pants

Box 4— Scarves, belts, jewelry, honeymoon peignoir, etc.

Give Away

Be sure you give away things you're not using. Many people today have limited finances and can't afford some things. If you have clothes that you aren't wearing, give them to someone who will be able to use them. They'll be grateful to you, and you'll feel good about your giving.

A   Clothing can be given to friends or family.

B   Clothing can also be given to thrift shops, Goodwill type stores, rummage sales, church, or missionaries.

C. You may want to have a garage sale with friends or a clothes sale.

Throw Away

Put these items in a trash bag with a twistie on it and set out for the trash.

HELPFUL HINTS

- When one leg in your panty hose gets a bad run, but the other is still okay, cut off the bad leg just below the panty part. Use it with another pair that has the same problem and you have saved a pair of panty hose.

- After wearing leather shoes, let them air out overnight before placing them in a shoebox and storing on the shelf. To maximize the use of your shoes, you need to rotate two or three pairs.

🍎 WARDROBE INVENTORY 🍎

Blouses	Pants	Skirts

Jackets	Sweaters	Dresses

Gowns	Lingerie	Shoes

Jewelery	

Things I Never Wear	Things I Need

9

Don't Be a Paperwork Slave

So you are no longer a slave, but a son;
and since you are a son,
God has made you also an heir.

Galatians 4:7, NIV

❧ —— ❧

I n *Survival for Busy Women,* I give a more detailed
offering of what to do with all the paper that comes
into your home and office.

If you can't get on top of paperwork, it will absolutely
bury you and make you feel overwhelmed. Here are a
few time-savers.

Control Junk Mail

In our home my Bob opens and controls the mail flow.
In your home you may be the one doing this. When you
go through the mail each day (I stress the *each day*—work
through today's mail before tomorrow's mail arrives),
have a recycle bin or trash can nearby. Get in the habit of
quickly deciding what goes in the trash. Don't procrastinate.

Place Mail to Review in One Folder

Bob places the folder behind our bed pillows and this
becomes our reading for the night. (This won't work for

all families, but for ours it does.) Have a trash can near the bed so you can toss the rejects into the container. The magazines go onto the living room coffee table, and last month's magazines go into a large antique toolbox for future storing and reading.

Personal Mail Goes to the Person

When the children were home, all personal mail went into the folder of each individual member of the Barnes family and went directly to the person's work station. This might be a desk, a kitchen table, or his or her bed. This way we all could find our daily mail.

File All Those Important Papers

Somewhere in your office area (wherever that might be), set up a simple or elaborate file system to keep all those important tax records, health insurance, life insurance, and auto insurance papers. This area could include storage of papers detailing information about that favorite someday vacation, car records, childhood doctor references, pet information, etc.

Don't Put It Down, Put It Away

One of the stresses of paper is that we put it down and have piles all over the house. Have a designated area for all papers. If you don't have one, make one.

Use Accordion Files

These are wonderful in that they have many versatile uses—all the way from storing bills for future payment to storing important papers and greeting and thank-you cards. You can set the files up with labels for each heading, along with "Pay," "Read," "Answer," "Pending," "Hold," etc. Some ladies even have one accordion file labeled for each month, and they go there the first thing each day and look in that day's slot to see what needs to be done.

Plastic Business-Card Holder

We all get business cards from the mechanic, painter, electrician, and life-insurance representative. Don't toss the cards in a drawer or drop them in your purse. Go directly to a stationery store and purchase a plastic business-card holder that will fit into your daily planner. The next time you get a business card, just file it away (if you think you will be using the person's services).

Use a Master Family Calendar

Each family needs its "control center" where all members of the family can go to see what's happening in the family. A bulletin board or a large monthly calendar can be posted on the refrigerator. It is a place for all announcements. It's a place to jot down all important notices—including birthdays and anniversaries.

Controlling paper will go a long way in determining how you will control other time-related parts of your life.

Don't become stressed out in this area. Continue to be alert to tools that will help you be better organized. Proper tools are very important. There are so many handy gadgets and containers that will assist you in your climb up this big mountain.

10

Stress Relievers

*Let no unwholesome word proceed
from your mouth, but only such a word
as is good for edification according
to the need of the moment, that it may
give grace to those who hear.*

Ephesians 4:29, NASB

᷿ —— ᷿

Are you late for appointments, pay the gas bill twice, don't send in tax payments on time (and have to pay interest along with a large penalty), forget luncheon engagements with dear friends, and even miss connecting flights because you were busy talking to a new friend in the coffee shop?

Organized families know how to avoid these stresses. And when we do, we certainly have happier family relationships. Let's look at a few stress busters, so we too can be stressed less because we are growing in organizational skills.

Stress Reducers at Home

- Mend only on one scheduled day a week. Put out a central box for family members can deposit garments for repairs. As the children get older, teach them how to mend their own garments.
- Get in the habit of using mats on both sides of entry doors. These will really cut down on dirt

accumulations in the home. This means less mop-
ping, less vacuuming, and less cleaning each
week.

- Members of the family need to help Mom keep
  their areas clean. Don't weaken and do it for them.
- When making repairs around the home and you
  aren't sure you'll remember how the parts go back
  together, draw a simple diagram. If you have a
  Polaroid camera, take a picture.
- Write chores on small slips of paper and put them
  into a small dish. Let the various members of the
  family draw out a slip and that becomes their
  chore for the next week. Even go one step further
  and write the name of the family member on a list
  alongside the chore he or she has drawn.
- Make sure that each bedroom has a clothes hamper or other laundry container so that each person
  can toss clothing into it, rather than on the floor.
  On the way to breakfast, have each person put the
  dirty clothes in a larger hamper in the wash area.

Speed-Ups for Procrastinators

- If your friend is usually 15 minutes late, tell her
  your meeting is 15 minutes earlier than normal.
- Set your household clock five to ten minutes
  ahead of the correct time. Don't tell anyone.
- Call the office of your next appointment to make
  sure they're running on schedule for your appointment.
- Rather than nag your children five minutes before
  they leave for school, church, or an activity, set a
  small alarm clock to go off five minutes before
  they are to leave (the oven clock works well, too).
- If you have a friend who is always late, call the

person a few hours before your appointment and confirm the time and place.

- Make a "To Do" list before going to bed or before leaving the office. Now you have a list of where to begin tomorrow.

Make Shopping a Piece of Cake

- Shop early in the morning or late at night (avoid peak hours).
- Shop from a grocery list. Get in and out of the market. This will also save you a lot of money.
- Write your shopping list on the back of an envelope and place inside the envelope only those coupons which deal with items you are going to buy.
- Avoid shopping for food when you are hungry or with your children.
- Take a small hand calculator with you to compare unit costs and to keep a running subtotal of your costs.
- Shop by mail order. This has been a real time- and money-saver for us.
- When shopping for clothes, wear garments which are easy to remove, with a minimum of buttons and zippers.
- Don't shop with negative people. They won't let you purchase anything because nothing is right.
- Tie a ribbon to your auto antenna when you aren't familiar with a parking lot so that your car will stand out. If you don't have an antenna that stays up, at least pick a landmark, a light post, a sign or an aisle number.
- Have extra household goods in the closet or pantry. When you run out, you have a backup to use.

These backups will save a lot of unnecessary trips at most unwelcome times.

Peacekeepers for Others

- Attach a list of most-used addresses to the back of your stationery box. Better yet, keep your small organizer close by so you have the addresses readily available.
- Limit travel to nonbusy times of the year. Stay away from holiday travel, if at all possible.
- When you make an appointment, write it on your calendar along with the person's telephone number.
- Teach the children how to select their own clothes for tomorrow's activities.
- Insist that all members of the family talk decently to each other. Encourage only positive remarks (see Ephesians 4:29).
- Limit intimate friends to a number you can handle properly. More than that creates added stress in your life.

TVs and Telephones Can Waste a Lot of Time

- Limit the amount of time you spend on the telephone with each caller.
- Turn your TV off at meal time (soft background music is very satisfying).
- Ignore the phone when it rings at mealtime. Use your answering machine to pick up any messages. Turn the ringer off during these times.
- TV and homework don't mix.
- Schedule at least two "no-TV" nights each week. These are times to read, communicate, get to know good music, play games, put puzzles together, etc.

- Don't accept any telephone solicitations. Tell callers to send a letter stating their company's request and background. (You probably will never receive it.)
- When you are limited on time, call the people you need to talk to when they won't be home, and leave a short message on their answering machine.

Stress Reducers

- Color-code that special key on your key chain so you don't have to continually search for that one key. Use bright nail polish.
- Color-code your extension cords when you have several at one outlet. This way you don't have to plug and unplug to see which cord goes where.
- Put waxed paper between ice cube trays to prevent them from freezing together.
- Keep an inventory of clothes you need for the next winter or summer. In the in-between months, look for the items when they go on sale.
- Keep an extra pair of panty hose in your desk at the office or in the trunk of your car.
- Sew extra buttons for your clothing on the inside or at the bottom of the garment. This way you know where to look when it needs mending.
- Have a fully equipped emergency kit in the back of your car.
- Tape the extra screws that come with furniture to the underside of chairs, sofas, and tables. They are there when you need them.
- Have a key hook in the kitchen where family members place keys when they come into the house. This saves a lot of time looking for keys.

Prevent Yourself from Losing Time

- If you have to remember something in the morning, tape a message to the front door or to your bathroom mirror.
- Write down addresses and telephone numbers in pencil. You can erase and rewrite them very easily.
- Put your daily pills in a plastic box marked for each day of the week. A quick glance tells you if you took your pills that day.
- Buy a couple pairs of reading glasses if you are someone who loses glasses often.
- Write down phone numbers, directions, and messages in a notebook that you take with you.
- Get an inexpensive cellular telephone—great for all those emergencies.
- Don't wait until your car's gasoline tank is almost empty to refill.
- Keep a blanket, jumper cables, hose clamps, flares, a sweater, an old pair of shoes, and a flashlight in the trunk of your car.
- Clean out your purse at least once a month so you don't waste time looking for whatever you keep in that big purse.

11

Feel Safe When You Travel

"'Sirs, what must I do to be saved?'
They replied, 'Believe in the Lord Jesus,
and you will be saved—you
and your household.'"

Acts 16:30,31, NIV

ઢ —— ઢ

As we open the newspapers or turn on the television, we are bombarded with terrible news all over the world regarding citizens being attacked violently. What can we do to protect ourselves and our families?

Our first priority is to be secure, and our verse for today gives us a glimpse of where that security comes from—the Lord Jesus Christ. He is our protector and defender. However, we are to do our part in keeping safe.

The following ideas will help you as you travel.

Foil Car Thieves

Car thieves look for easy jobs. Their most attractive quarry, of course, is a car with the keys left in it. That's how 40 percent of thefts occur. Car thieves also like dark and secluded parking places, and cars with keys hidden in those little magnetic boxes. Theives are especially fond of unlocked doors and windows, and get access to 80 percent of their loot that way. *Always* lock your car and take the keys with you.

- *Protect your car keys.* Most car keys have an identification number printed on them. Have your car dealer or locksmith punch out those numbers, and keep a record of the numbers in a safe place, in case you need a duplicate.

- *Get a "credit-card key."* This credit-card key is made of metal-reinforced plastic with an outline of your key, which you can pop out and use if you lock yourself out of your car. Because you carry this key with you in your wallet, it is *much* safer than the magnetic box that burglars find so helpful. Ask for one wherever you get your keys made.

- *Park in attended lots.* If you park in an unattended parking lot, your car is five times more likely to be stolen than if you park on the street or in an attended lot. When we lived in New York, we had to figure these exorbitant parking lot fees into the cost of a day trip into the Big Apple.

  When you park your car in a lot with a valet service, remove your house keys from your key ring or give the valet a key chain with only your car keys. Ideally, you shouldn't leave anything of value in the car. However, if you can't take items with you, hide your valuables in your trunk.

- *Etch your Social Security number* or driver's license number on your tape deck, CB radio, cellular phone, and several places on the car for easy identification.

- *Keep a record of your vehicle identification number* in a safe place. Trucks and RVs don't always have a number, so mark these vehicles with your own code number, such as your Social Security number.

- *Don't leave your driver's license or other identification in the car,* and keep your registration and insurance papers out of sight. In high-crime areas, consider taking these papers out of your car.

- *Park with your wheels turned sharply to the curb,* to make towing difficult.

- *Conceal valuable stereo equipment, cellular phones, and radar detectors.* You can use some simple camouflage, such as black cardboard taped on the dash, or get a more elaborate built-in concealment system. You can also get stereo components that have concealment features.

- *Get your bearings before you drive in new towns.* When you're in a strange town, ask the hotel concierge, tourist information office, or police department if there are unsafe areas that you should not drive in. If you must drive through them, keep your windows up and doors locked.

- *Get a car alarm system* to frighten off thieves with sirens, horns, lights—or all three. You can also get a portable alarm system for use in more than one car.

- *Get other car protection devices.* You can also protect your car with these devices: a gas-tank lock, a fuel switch that keeps fuel from entering the carburetor, a kill switch that keeps electrical current from the coil or distributor, interior hood locks, a "J-Bar" steering wheel lock, and locks such as "Lasso Lock" that secure your stereo equipment.

- *Consider public transportation.* Many areas are so congested with autos and people that driving a car isn't practical. Besides, public transportation gives you a better opportunity to sightsee. Traveling independently is a lot more fun than traveling in groups; however, there is safety in numbers.

Increase Your Personal Safety

Whether you're going on a tour or traveling independently, don't let the pleasure and relaxation of travel make you careless about your own safety. When you set out, leave your valuables behind. You'll be less attractive to thieves, and you won't risk losing your belongings.

Weed out your wallet. Don't take credit cards and other material you won't need. Wrap a rubber band around your wallet and keep it in your inside pocket. Some travel stores have special clamps to secure your wallet in your pocket. Another option is to carry your money in a money belt, leaving just enough money in your wallet for the day's activities. If possible, wear clothing with secure pockets, and don't take any more than you can carry in them.

For women, it's best to carry no purse at all. Even if you are hiding your purse under a jacket and holding on tight, it can be snatched by a swift motorcyclist. If you must take a purse, make it a fanny pack.

Make a note of your traveler's check numbers, and photocopy your passport identification pages, driver's license, and all credit cards you're taking with you. Give copies to a friend, and tuck other copies in your wallet and luggage.

Use Precautions at the Airport

Be very vigilant as you enter an airport. Pickpockets thrive on the crowds and confusion in the entrance areas, so get past security checks and into the waiting area as soon as possible. Get your boarding pass in advance, if you can.

We try to limit ourselves to carry-on luggage, so we don't have to fight through the baggage-claim area. If you do check luggage, make sure it's securely locked and easy to identify. If we have to check baggage through, we wind colorful wool yarn or a bright ribbon around the handles so no one will claim our bags by mistake.

If you use your home address on luggage tags, get tags that have a flap to conceal the information from casual observers. It's better to use a post office box number or office address. Have this information inside your suitcase as well. Add a small combination lock to your suitcase for added security from pilfering baggage handlers.

Find out in advance about ground transportation from the airport to help you ward off unscrupulous drivers and guides.

Beef Up Your Hotel Safety

When you check into a hotel, book a room between the second and seventh floor. You'll have more protection from burglars than if you were on the ground floor, and you'll still be low enough for fire equipment to reach you in an emergency. Read the emergency directions in your room. Locate the nearest fire exit, and count the doors between your room and the exit. Other hotel safety tips include:

- Keep airline tickets, unneeded traveler's checks and other valuables in a hotel safe-deposit box.

- Meet new acquaintances in the lobby, and don't give them your room number.

International Travel

- Make a note of emergency numbers, including police, fire, your hotel, and the U.S. embassy and consulate. Learn how to use the pay phones, and have change handy.

- Learn enough of your host country's language to be able to communicate your need for assistance.

Take the Worry Out of Sightseeing

Before you set out on your sight-seeing trips, ask your concierge, tour leader, or local police department which neighborhoods you should avoid, and what (if any) special precautions you need to take to protect yourself.

In high-crime locations, dress casually and look confident. Don't let yourself be distracted by muggers working in pairs. Walk in the middle of the sidewalk, away from doorways and streets. If someone does accost you, give the person what he wants. In my mind, *nothing* is as valuable as *your life and your safety.*

Of course, many areas of the United States and foreign countries are quite safe and welcoming to visitors. One of the joys of travel is meeting new people, and you can usually trust your instincts on when and where you can open up to new friends and experiences. If you fortify yourself against the possible dangers, you'll be able to relax in the far-more-numerous safe environments.

If you take the necessary steps to keep your property and yourself reasonably safe, you can enjoy your travels without fear and with maximum enjoyment.

Travel Resources

- *Cole Consumer Products* (31100 Solon Rd., Solon, OH 44139; (216) 248-7000)—a good source for credit card keys.

- *Magellan's* (P.O. Box 5485, Santa Barbara, CA 93150; (800) 962-4943)—a travel gear mail-order house.

- *The Safe Travel Book: A Guide for International Travelers* (Free Press; $12.95).

- For foreign travel get information from embassies and/or consulates of the various countries you will be visiting. Call *Citizens Emergency Center*, (202) 647-5225.

- *101 Tips For Mature Travelers* is available free from Grand Circle Travel, (800) 248-3737. This guide includes helpful tips on exchange rates, metric conversions, and an overseas tipping guide.[1]

12

Air Travel: The Perils of Packing

*And if I go and prepare a place for you,
I will come again, and receive
you to Myself; that where I am,
there you may be also.*

John 14:3, NASB

❧ —— ❧

What do the following items have in common:

- A totem pole
- A vacuum cleaner
- A refrigerator
- A foreign-car drive shaft
- A kitchen sink?

You can't figure it out? Then you haven't been flying lately.

Airline personnel recount that these are actual items that people have brought to the airport and attempted to cart on board as carry-on luggage. Hard to believe, but true.

How can you know what to pack, where to pack, or whether to even pack an item at all? What you can bring is defined quite specifically. You are allowed the following as carry-on luggage:

- Toiletries
- Medical articles
- Carbon dioxide gas cylinders worn by passengers to operate mechanical limbs
- Dry ice for packing perishables (may not exceed four pounds)
- Electric wheelchairs
- Unloaded firearms in a locked container checked with an airline representative and small arms ammunition securely packaged in material designed for transporting ammunition
- Matches and lighters

Unfortunately, most violators don't find out about the irregularities until they arrive at the airport. Usually that's too late, and irritation occurs.

American Airlines has printed a few basic do's and don'ts for their passengers. Some of these tips are:

- Pack smart and keep valuables like jewelry and cameras in your hand luggage.
- Put baggage tags both inside and outside the bag.
- Leave for the airport early. Allow for car trouble and overcrowded street traffic near the airport.
- Check the routing of your baggage. Make sure the agent or skycap attaches the correct tags for your destination city.
- Abide by the amount of carryons you are allowed. (Check with your airline—each varies.)

As a general rule, airlines limit the number of carryons to one per passenger with dimensions not exceeding 21″

x 15" x 9". Most planes also have closets to hang garment bags.

Many international governments are very specific. Usually there are guidelines that say something like "No more carry-on luggage can be brought on board than can be safely stowed." All this really means is that it depends on the individual airline as well as the particular type of aircraft that will be used on your flight.

Always check with your individual airline *before* you head for the airport as to its specific baggage rules. Use common sense when all else fails.

Here are some ideas on what to check in, what to carry on, and what to leave at home.

For Your Carry-on Bag

- Any prescription medicine you take, along with photocopies of the prescription itself

- A photocopy of your airline tickets, your itinerary, and (if traveling overseas) your passport

- A small supply of replacement batteries for any electronic items you'll be using on your flight

- An inflatable neck pillow

- Reading material

- A casual pair of warm-ups (in case your check-in luggage is late)

- Stationery—in-flight time is great for getting caught up on your thank-you notes and long-overdue letters.

For Check-in Bags

- A basic personal medicine kit

- A small umbrella

- A voltage converter plug and adapter kit for hair dryers and shavers (overseas flights only)

- Plastic bags for dirty items and shoes

- Girth belts for luggage. You don't want to have to depend solely on the often-flimsy locks and zippers on luggage (particularly if you are like most of us and overstuff your suitcase).

- An extra plastic or canvas bag for the stuff you can't fit in your checked-in bags on your return flight

- A small battery-operated alarm clock. You need a backup for the front desk attendant who forgets to wake you up. (You don't want to oversleep on the day of departure for home.)

- A small flashlight—for those little emergencies

- If you wear glasses, a repair kit is a must. Make sure it has a small screwdriver and small screws.

- Additional replacement batteries for all the high-tech gadgets you are taking along. (Gift stores are very expensive.)

- Additional film for your camera

By following these hints, you should have a more enjoyable trip. Don't forget to kiss your spouse, children, and animals before you leave. They will miss you while you're gone.

13

Prayer Organization

*Admit your faults to one another
and pray for each other
so that you may be healed.*

James 5:16

❧ —— ❧

Some of you may not have a prayer life at all. Others of you may have a very vital prayer life. Some of you want to have a prayer life but are fumbling with it because you don't know how to incorporate it into your life or how to organize it. I was once in that position. I was fumbling in my prayer life because I didn't know the steps to take. That's what we want to discuss now—some steps to take in order to set up a prayer notebook and to organize our prayer life.

One Set of Footprints

One night a man had a dream. In his dream he was walking along the beach with the Lord, when across the sky flashed all the events of his life. However, for each scene he noticed two sets of footprints in the sand, one belonging to him and the other to the Lord. When the last scene had flashed before him, he looked back at the footprints and noticed that many times along the path there was only one set of footprints in the sand. He also noticed that this happened during the lowest and saddest times of his life.

This really bothered him, so he said to the Lord, "You promised that once I decided to follow You, You would walk with me all the way, but I noticed that during the roughest times of my life there was only one set of footprints. I don't understand why You deserted me when I needed You the most."

The Lord replied, "My precious child, I love you and I would never leave you. During those times of trial and suffering when you saw only one set of footprints, it was then that I carried you."

You see, God is always with us. When the times are the lowest, that's when He picks us up and carries us. Isn't that wonderful? Some of us have experienced that. Some of us right now are in a position where we're being carried through a rough situation or problem in our life. It's wonderful to know that we have our Lord there in order to carry us when times get low and things get rough.

Often we don't take the necessary time with our Lord in prayer and communication. But do you know what? He loves us anyway. He loves us unconditionally. And that's why we need to pull together some type of system in our lives where we can spend valuable time in prayer. It doesn't have to be long, either. Sometimes we get turned off because we feel it takes so much time, but it doesn't have to be long.

How to Get Started

As with everything else, we need the proper tools and materials. I would recommend a small notebook, perhaps a 5½" x 8½" three-ring binder. Get some colored tabs, some paper, some dividers, and a pen.

Be sure to have your Bible handy. Sometimes you may want to do a little Bible study with yourself as you go into your prayer time, so it's always nice to have your Bible with you. As I pray, I find that many times God reveals something to me in His Word. If I'm praying for someone, I sometimes feel really impressed to drop that person a note and tell him I'm praying for him, supporting him. At times like this I like to be able to give a Bible verse, so it's nice to have my Bible close by.

Colossians 4:2 (NASB) says that we are to "devote [ourselves] to prayer, keeping alert in it with an attitude of thanksgiving." Our attitude as we come to the Lord should be one of thanksgiving. Christ is waiting for us. His attitude toward us is love. And our attitude in return should be one of thanksgiving.

Why Should We Pray?

Why do we pray? We pray because we want to communicate with God. In Luke 18:1 Jesus said that people ought to pray always, without giving up. Prayer also gives us an opportunity to confess to God those things that we feel guilty about. First John 1:9 says, "If we confess our sins to him, he can be depended on to forgive us and to cleanse us from every wrong." We can open our heart to God and confess the very worst things in our lives down to the very smallest things. God hears us, and nobody else has to know those things. This begins to teach us discipline. When we pray we're disciplined in knowing that we are in the hand of God and that God is there to touch us, to feed us, and to give us what He wants us to have. This draws us closer to the Lord. As we begin to pray even briefly, we begin to draw on that fellowship that we have with Christ.

Prayer keeps us from being selfish. It keeps us from looking at ourselves and the things *we* want. When we begin to pray for someone else, we remove ourselves from "me" and we focus on the other person, to love the other person. Prayer also keeps us from temptation and disobedience to God. As we pray we draw closer to God, and as we draw closer to God, we find that we want to do what God wants for us. We want to be the women that God wants us to be.

How We Should Pray

Luke 22:41 says that Jesus knelt and began to pray. This doesn't mean that every time you pray you have to get on your knees, though there are times when you will want to do this. Be flexible. We have a tendency to think that we have to keep asking God for something over and over, but Matthew 6:7 says, "Don't recite the same prayer over and over." We can give our needs to God without constantly reminding Him of them, since He already knows all about them. So if we don't pray for that thing every day, God still knows. We may pray for it once a week or once a month.

A woman I met in Newport Beach had prayed for her husband for 35 years. I'm sure she didn't get down on her knees every day and pray fervently for her husband for 15 minutes for 35 years. But she was in an attitude of prayer for 35 years, and then one day when her husband was in his seventies he received Christ and stepped into the kingdom of God. God hears our prayers!

The Right Approach

As we approach God in prayer we first need to praise Him, to adore Him, to thank Him for all the things He has given us and just for who He is. This is better than asking God immediately for all the things we want.

Then we need to confess our sins and shortcomings to God, opening up our heart and talking freely to God.

We should be willing to thank God for everything. Our attitude should be one of thankfulness. If we're depressed, we should thank God for even the smallest things. As we begin to make a list of the things that we're thankful for, our selfishness will begin to disappear.

Then we need to submit ourselves to God. He wants to hear our needs and our supplications. Matthew 7:7,8 (NASB) says, "Ask, and it shall be given to you; seek, and you shall find; knock, and it shall be opened to you. For everyone who asks receives, and he who seeks finds, and to him who knocks it shall be opened." God *wants* to answer our prayers and to give us the desires of our heart.

Make a List

When you organize your prayer notebook, you need to make a list of the things you would like to pray for. For example, you could have a section for your family. Then you could have personal prayer requests. These could include such things as financial needs or a situation between you and your husband.

You should also have a section in your notebook for your church, including your pastor and his wife and family. All of us should pray for the rulers of our country, our state, and our city. If you have children in school, you should pray for the principal and all the teachers, plus the friends that your children have at school.

Then, of course, you should pray for yourself. Pray that you can begin to incorporate some of the organization that we've talked about. Pray for your personal needs. You may be struggling with anger toward someone or selfishness.

You need to pray for your husband. It is important that you uphold him in prayer. He's out there working, struggling in the world, trying to make a living. Situations and circumstances come into his life that require you to uphold him and support him in prayer.

And then, of course, we need to pray for our missionaries as they spread God's Word to many different people throughout the world in areas that we ourselves cannot reach.

Keeping Track

As we take this list of items that we're to pray for, we delegate them in our notebook to our little tabs. The tabs will be labeled with each day of the week. This is the easiest way I have found to set up a prayer notebook. So you have Monday, Tuesday, Wednesday, Thursday, Friday, Saturday, and Sunday tabs.

Behind the Monday tab you might put your family prayer requests, listing those people in your family that you're to pray for. When Monday morning comes and you have your little quiet time with the Lord, you pray for those needs. You know they're being covered at least once a week. (Of course, you can pray for them at other times as well.)

Tuesday might be your prayer day for your country, your church, your pastor, and maybe your Bible study. Bob and I teach a Tuesday night couples' Bible study. We have under my Tuesday tab the needs of the couples in our study. During the study I list the prayer requests that are given. This way I can look on the page and see that, for example, Peter doesn't have a job. So I pray for Peter. Then when Peter gets a job I say, "Thank You, Lord, for giving Peter a job." (Always date your prayer requests and answers.)

Saturday is a difficult day, so I pray for miscellaneous requests. Sometimes on Saturday you may not even get a chance to pray. Your children are home, your schedule is off, and you're going on picnics and so forth. Keep Saturday open.

On Sunday, instead of having a list of people I pray for, I outline the sermons. I find that if I'm writing, I'm listening better, and I'm able to understand the sermon better and digest it better. I also find that people come to me with prayer requests at church on Sunday. I write these in my prayer notebook on Sunday, and I pray for them on Monday, Tuesday, Wednesday, or Thursday as I'm going through my time of prayer during the week.

God Hears Children, Too

Give your children an opportunity to share in prayer with you also. Let them give you some prayer requests. Bob and I started doing this when our children were in high school. Since breakfast was the only meal of the day when we would gather together as a family, we would share with one another at that time. For example: "What kind of exam are you going to have?" After we got together again, we would always have a point of reference: "How did your exam go?" They might say to me, "How did your speaking go?" Or they might ask, "How was your job today? Did you get the project done that you were working on?" This way prayer requests become part of our lives.

When to Pray

When should we pray? The morning is an important time to pray. Maybe we can pray in a private place in our home, or maybe it can be somewhere else. I spend a lot of time in my car, and I find this a valuable time to spend in prayer. People look at me on the street or the freeways and wonder why nobody else is in the car and my mouth is moving. But I'm talking to my Lord. Be sure not to close your eyes when you're driving and praying!

We also need to pray with other people. Matthew 18:20 (NASB) says, "Where two or three have gathered together in My name, there I am in their midst." As we pray together, we don't need to make our prayers long, praying for everything in the world and everything in our notebook. I have found that women who pray that way generally don't have good prayer times by themselves at home because they spend so much time when they're with someone else with long, flowery prayers. God doesn't care about our words; He only cares about our attitude.

We can pray short prayers in our Bible study group, in our prayer group, or over the telephone. Often people call me with a problem and I say, "Let's pray." This is a wonderful way to spend some time on the phone. I don't have a lot of time for deep conversation on the phone, but I take the time to say, "Let's pray about it. I don't know all the details of your situation, and you don't have to spell them all out to me, but God knows all about them, so let's pray about it."

The Desires of Our Hearts

God is interested in the desires of our hearts, even those where we think, "I'd love to have it, but I'm afraid to ask because it may seem selfish or even a little silly." It's the *attitude* toward those things that He's really concerned about.

Check yourself by saying, "Lord, if it wouldn't be good for me to have these things, then I really don't want them. But if it would be okay with You, I'd be very grateful and would use them for Your glory." Your list could include a lot of things; these are prayer wishes. Maybe it's a new sofa, or the women's overnight retreat that you can't attend because you don't have the finances.

I have a friend whose curling iron went out, but she didn't have enough money to buy a new one. She went into a beauty supply store and told the man that she didn't have any money but needed a curling iron. He replied, "Don't worry about it—we have one that was brought back because the lady didn't want that size. She didn't have it in the right box, so you can have it." My friend couldn't believe that God was even interested in her curling iron!

Remember to thank God for all things, because He is interested in all things. Ephesians 5:20 says, "Always give thanks for everything . . . in the name of our Lord Jesus Christ." God is interested in the desires of our hearts.

PRAYER ORGANIZATION SUMMARY

"Devote yourselves to prayer, keeping alert in it with an attitude of thanksgiving."
(Colossians 4:2, NASB)

Materials Needed

- Small three-ring binder with front pocket
- Paper
- Seven dividers with tabs
- Pen
- Bible

Why Pray?

A. We pray because our Lord prayed: *"He walked away, perhaps a stone's throw, and knelt down and prayed this prayer: 'Father, if you are willing, please take away this cup of horror from me. But I want your will, not mine.' Then an angel from heaven appeared and strengthened him, for he was in such agony of spirit that he broke into a sweat of blood, with great drops falling to the ground as he prayed more and more earnestly. At last he stood up again and returned to the disciples—only to find them asleep, exhausted from grief"* (Luke 22:41-45).

B. Prayer gives us the opportunity for confession.

C. Prayer brings discipline to our lives.

D. Prayer draws us closer to our Lord.

E. Praying for others keeps us from selfishness.

F. Prayer helps us to love those we have difficulty loving.

G. Prayer keeps us from disobedience to God and temptations.

> *"God...will provide*
> *the way of escape."*
> (1 Corinthians 10:13, NASB)

> *"Pray God that you will not fall*
> *when you are tempted."*
> (Luke 22:46)

How to Pray

> *"He knelt down and began to pray."*
> (Luke 22:41, NASB)

A. *"Don't recite the same prayer over and over as the heathen do, who think prayers are answered only by repeating them again and again. Remember, your Father knows exactly what you need even before you ask him!"* (Matthew 6:7,8).

B. A Helpful Reminder:

A—Adore God.
C—Confess to God.
T—Thank God for everything.
S—Supplication and submission unto God.

C. *"Ask, and it shall be given to you; seek, and you shall find; knock, and it shall be opened to you. For everyone who asks receives, and he who seeks finds, and to him who knocks it shall be opened"* (Matthew 7:7,8, NASB).

What to Pray For

A. Make a list of all needs:

1. Family (children, in-laws, etc.)

2. Personal (finances, problems)

3. Friends

4. Church (pastor and his family, church leaders)

5. Country (city, state, president, etc.)

6. School (teachers, principal, students)

7. Husband (work, etc.)

8. Self (home, anger, organizing, etc.)

9. Missionaries

Delegate the above to a day of the week, Monday through Saturday (use tabs).

B. Sunday's tab will be used for sermon outlines and prayer requests.

1. Prayer requests will be added to the above categories.

2. Date prayer requests and date God's answers. Answers may be "wait" ("not now"), "no," or "yes." Always give thanks.

C. Let the children give prayer requests. *"All things you ask in prayer, believing, you shall receive"* (Matthew 21:22, NASB).

When to Pray

- Morning
- Noon
- Evening
- Meals
- Bedtime

Where to Pray

> *"When you pray, go into your inner room,*
> *and when you have shut your door,*
> *pray to your Father who is in secret,*
> *and your Father who sees*
> *in secret will repay you."*
> (Matthew 6:6, NASB)

A. Home—in the closet; while doing dishes, vacuuming, cleaning

B. In the car; while jogging, exercising, walking

C. With others—*"Where two or three have gathered together in My name, there I am in their midst"* (Matthew 18:20, NASB).

   1. Bible study groups

   2. Women's prayer groups

   3. With a girlfriend

   4. On the phone with a friend

Wish Prayers

A. God already knows the desires of our hearts, and He wants us to ask Him for them. It's the *attitude* about those things that He is concerned about.

B. Check yourself by saying, "Lord, if it wouldn't be good for me to have this, then I really don't want it. But if it would be okay with You, I'll be very grateful and use it for Your glory."

C. Be prepared—God always answers. It may be an immediate "yes," a "wait awhile," an absolute "no," or "the timing is not right at present." Record these answers in your notebook by the item, and allow God to work in your life with His love in giving you what's best for your life. Remember to thank Him in all things. *"Always giving thanks for all things in the name of our Lord Jesus Christ"* (Ephesians 5:20, NASB).

Part

2

*More Hours...
and Home
Organization*

14

Total Mess to Total Rest

If you wait for perfect conditions,
you will never get anything done.

Ecclesiastes 11:4

ε ——— ε

S uppose I were to say to you, "Today, I'm going to come home with you. I want you to take me into your house, and I want to go through your closets, to look under your bed, to open your drawers, to look in your pantry, and to go anyplace in your house. I just want to check out your house really well."

Some of you would reply, "Well, that's okay. I've got my house in order, and things are really good there, so you can come over." Others of you would say, "Okay, but don't go into the third bedroom, because I've been shoving things in that back bedroom for a long time. That's my little hideaway. You can't go back there, but you can look everywhere else." Still others of you might say, "There is no way anybody is going to come into my house, because the whole place is a total mess."

Controlling Your Home

I am going to show you how to take that mess, no

matter what size it is, and turn it into a home that you'll be able to maintain and be able to rest in. You will control your home instead of your home controlling you.

Here's some of the equipment you'll need in order to work out this program. You'll need three to ten boxes 16" deep x 12" wide by 10" high with lids. (I call these "Perfect Boxes.") You'll need a 3" x 5" card-file box and some 3" x 5" cards. Get ten cards in each color—blue, yellow, pink, white, green, orange, cherry. Be sure to get some little tabs for each section of cards, and also a pen to write on them. Then you'll need at least ten colored file folders. (I like to use the colored ones because they help to identify things.) If you already have a metal file cabinet at home, that's great, but most people don't have one. The file boxes are a lot less expensive.

I've been teaching my seminars for several years now, and after about the first six months I discovered something about us women. Our intentions are good and we want to get started, but somehow we can't seem to get organized enough to get ourselves organized, and we just throw the whole program out the window. So pray about the program. Ask God to make you willing to get the materials and to incorporate them into your home. (See page 343 for information on ordering the materials.)

Commit Yourself

You'll want to commit yourself to five weeks in taking that total mess and cleaning it up. I don't want you to become overwhelmed thinking about it, because you're going to take a small portion at a time—only one room a week for the next five weeks. You'll do it nice and slow, so that you'll gradually get your home under control.

It can all be done in 15-minute time slots. On Monday, go into Room 1 and clean like mad for 15 minutes, then forget it until Tuesday and do the same as you did

Monday, spending 15 minutes cleaning and organizing. Continue this process throughout the week. Presto! By the end of the week you will have spent one hour and 30 minutes in Room 1. You'll still have Sunday off and a nice, clean, well-organized room. Continue this process until every room in the house is complete.

We're going to take three large boxes or, if you prefer, three large trash bags. I like the trash bags because they're lightweight and you can drag them through the house. So take your three trash bags and label one of them "Put Away," one "Throw Away," and one "Give Away." I suggest using black trash bags so you cannot see in them—and so your husband and children cannot see in the bags, either.

Now visualize yourself standing at the front door with these three big trash bags. Ring the doorbell, then walk through the front door. The first room you come to will be the first room you're going to clean, with the exception of the kitchen. (If that's the room you walk into first, move on. You'll save the kitchen till the fifth week, because you'll need all the experience you can get before tackling the kitchen. See chapter 19 for a detailed explanation of kitchen organization.) To make it easy, let's say we step into the living room, and on our right is the hall closet.

So we open up the hall closet. We're now going to take everything out of that hall closet. We have to decide to get vicious in making choices about what to do with all the stuff we've taken out of the hall closet. I recommend that you call a friend who would like to help you with your house (and you help with her house). It's great to have a friend because she'll help you make decisions that you haven't been able to make for 15 years. She'll tell you, "Throw it out or give it away," and that will be very helpful to you.

The Hall Closet

Let's put into the hall closet all those things which actually belong in a hall closet. These include sweaters, coats, umbrella, boots, football blanket, binoculars, tennis rackets, etc.

But now we have all these other things that don't belong in there, such as old magazines that we've collected for six or seven years. (We were going to look through them some rainy day and cut out the pictures and recipes, but we never did.) So we have to get rid of these things. We've also got papers and receipts and all sorts of other things in that hall closet, so we'll put these either in the Put Away bag, the Throw Away bag, or the Give Away bag.

As we go through our home every week for the next five weeks, we begin to fill up these bags. At the end of the fifth week we may have three, ten, or fifteen bags full of various things. Then we put twisties on the trash bags marked Throw Away and set them out for the trashman. Now they're gone! You've got all those things out of the way.

Now you have two types of bags left: the Give Away bags and the Put Away bags. The Give Away bags will hold things that you may want to hand down to some other family member or to relatives, or clothing that you want to give to a thrift shop, sell at a rummage sale, or donate to your church.

Maybe three or four of you who have done the five-week program will want to have a garage sale and make a little extra money. Buy something for yourself or for the house, or give the profits to your church or missionary group. Now you've cleaned these things out of your house and put them to good use in somebody else's hands.

Keeping It Neat

We have our house totally clean. How are we going to maintain it that way? We certainly never want to go through this total mess again! The cleanup lasted for five weeks, and we don't *have* to do it again.

The way we maintain our organized house is to take our 3″ x 5″ cards and label each of the divider tabs. The first color is going to be labeled "Daily." On these cards we list all those things that we have to do daily in our house in order to maintain it, such as washing the dishes and making the bed (plus all the other daily things).

The second section is those things we do weekly. For example, on Monday we wash; on Tuesday we iron and water the houseplants; on Wednesday we mop the floors; on Thursday we vacuum and do our marketing; and so on through the week.

Now Thursday comes along, and Sue, your very special friend, calls you and says, "Let's go to lunch and go shopping. The department store has a big sale today." So you check your cards and say, "I've done all my daily things, but it's Thursday, so I have to vacuum and go to the market. I can do my marketing this afternoon when we get back from lunch, but I don't know about the vacuuming."

So you go with Sue and get your bargains, but the vacuuming isn't done. So you decide to move the vacuuming over to Friday. But you look on Friday's card and see all those other things to do on Friday. So you take Friday's chores and move them to Saturday. But on Saturday you're going to the park with the kids. So you decide to move those things to *Sunday* now. But on Sunday you can't do them either because you're going to church and you've also got company coming afterward. So here we are going around in circles again. We've moved one job from day to day, but we're completely confused.

So we don't do that. Instead, on Thursday when we go to lunch with Sue and don't have time to vacuum, we move our vacuuming card to the back of the weekly section. This means we don't vacuum our house again until next Thursday, when the vacuuming card comes up in our file again. In other words, we rotate our cards daily whether we do the allotted jobs or not.

This means that we're crunching along on dirty carpet for a week or two. You say, "I can't possibly do that." But now you're disciplining yourself to keep your priorities in order. So next week when Sue calls and says, "Let's go to lunch," you tell her, "I'll go to lunch if I get my vacuuming done, because if I don't get it done today it means another whole week before I can do it." Remember, *you* want to be in control of your home, and not the other way around.

Next you have your monthly chores. During Week 1 you clean the refrigerator (you have a whole week to do it, or you can delegate the job to a child). During Week 2 you do the oven, and so forth. This way, every week you're doing a little bit to maintain your home. It's only going to take you a little time, but you're continually maintaining your home so you never have to go through that total mess program again. Next you have your quarterly things to do (straighten drawers, etc.). Then you have your semiannual tasks (rearrange furniture, wash curtains, etc.). Finally, there are the annual jobs such as cleaning the basement, attic, garage, etc.

Your last tab, at the very back of your file, is your storage tab. Here you take your 3" x 5" cards and number them Box 1, Box 2, Box 3, and so forth. Then you take your storage boxes that you've been collecting (or that you've purchased), line them all up, and number them Box 1, Box 2, Box 3, etc. You've got all these boxes in a row now, and a card that corresponds with each box.

If you want to go a step further, you can make out *two* cards for each box—one to be pasted on the box and one to go into your card file. Remember that Put Away bag, with Billy's first baby blanket, etc.? Well, you start putting these things into Box 1. Then you list on the 3" x 5" card labeled "Box 1" all the things which are actually in the box. And you do that with everything you find in those Put Away bags.

Maintaining Memories

A while ago our son, Brad, came home from college and said to Dad, "Remember when you used to referee those football and basketball games, and you wore that black-and-white striped shirt? Well, I'd like to wear it because we're going to have a black-and-white party at school and you can't get into this party unless you wear black and white. So I'd like to wear your shirt."

Bob looked at me and thought out loud, "I don't know where the shirt is. I haven't seen the shirt for 15 years." But I knew where the shirt was. I went right over to my card file, checked it out, and said, "Oh, yes, it's in Box 5." So I said to Brad and Bob, "Go out into the garage, look up on the shelf, find Box 5, pull it down, and inside that box you will find your black-and-white referee shirt." Sure enough, there it was, and Brad wore the shirt to the party!

Now as we take our file box and our colored file folders and look in that Put Away bag, what do we find? We find old newspaper clippings, warranties, instruction booklets, receipts from car repairs and household repairs, and all kinds of other things. So we put these papers in our colored file folders, label the folders, list all those things on 3" x 5" cards, and file the cards away in our file box.

Receipts Equal Money

Not long ago I had a neat experience. The icemaker on our refrigerator broke for the second time. When I called the repairman he said, "Mrs. Barnes, that's the same thing I fixed about six months ago." I asked, "How much will it cost?" He replied, "Sixty-five dollars. However, it's under warranty, if you can find the receipt."

Well, little did he know! I went right to my file, looked under Repair Receipts, and within 30 seconds had the receipt. I asked him, "Is this what you need?" He replied, "Yes, you've just saved yourself 65 dollars."

The Children's File Box

When our children were about 12 or 13 years old, I set up a file box for each of them. (I wish I had done it even earlier). I gave them ten file folders, and one day we went through the Total Mess program in their rooms. So they began to file all their report cards, all their special reports, and all their pictures and letters. Jenny was lucky enough to get some love letters, so she filed those in her file box. She also pressed and filed the flowers from her special dates and proms. When she got her first car, the insurance papers all went into the file box.

When the children went away to college, the first thing they took with them was their file box. It had all their important papers. When they came home for the summer, home came the file box. When Jenny and Craig were married in September, she took her file box with her. All her little treasures were in that box. Then she got another box and ten more file folders, and she set up a household file box. So now she has all those warranties, instruction booklets, and insurance papers in her household file.

What have we done? We've taken that total mess and changed it into total rest. And we'll maintain that rest. What does that give us? More hours in our day, with no guilt feelings about an unorganized house

TOTAL MESS TO
TOTAL REST SUMMARY

Equipment Needed

Three to ten "Perfect Boxes" with flip-top lids
3" x 5" card-file box
3" x 5" colored cards with dividers w/colored tabs
Twelve 8½" x 11" colored manila file folders

How to Get Organized

A. Begin by purchasing "Perfect Boxes" with flip-top lids.

B. Plan a five-week program project.

C. Label three large trash bags as follows:
   1. Put Away
   2. Throw Away
   3. Give Away

D. Start at your front door and go through your house, starting with the living room and ending with the kitchen.
   1. Closets, drawers, shelves.
   2. Get vicious!

Household Routine

A. Set up a 3" x 5" colored card-file box with dividers and tabs.

B. Label dividers in this card file as follows:

   1. Daily   5. Semiannually
   2. Weekly   6. Annually
   3. Monthly   7. Storage
   4. Quarterly

C. Make a list of jobs to be done:
   1. Daily

      a) dishes
      b) make beds
      c) clean bathrooms
      d) pick up rooms
      e) pick up kitchen

   2. Weekly:

      a) Monday—wash, grocery shopping
      b) Tuesday—iron, water plants
      c) Wednesday—mop floors
      d) Thursday—vacuum, go shopping
      e) Friday—change bed linens
      f) Saturday—do yard work
      g) Sunday—free except to plan for next week

NOTE: If you skip a job on an allotted day, *don't do it*. Put the card at the back of the file section and skip it until next week.

   3. Monthly:

      a. Week 1—Clean refrigerator
      b. Week 2—Clean oven
      c. Week 3—Mend clothing
      d. Week 4—Clean and dust baseboards throughout the home

   4. Quarterly:

      a. Clean drawers, windows
      b. Clean closets, move furniture and vacuum
      c. Clean china cabinets, cupboards, linen drawers

      Ask yourself, "How clean does my house have to be to meet the needs of my family?"

5. Semiannually:

    a. Clean screens
    b. Rearrange furniture
    c. Change filter in the furnace

6. Annually:

    a. Wash curtains
    b. Clean drapes
    c. Clean carpets
    d. Wash walls
    e. Clean out garage
    f. Touch up exterior paint
    g. Make repairs around the home

Storage

A. Get "Perfect Boxes" with flip-top lids and number each box Box 1, Box 2, Box 3, etc.

B. Assign each box a 3″ x 5″ card with a corresponding number. For example:

Box 1—a. Bill's baby clothes
        b. Bill's baby book
Box 2—Toys
Box 3—Seasonal clothes
Box 4—Fall decorations
Box 5—Books: high school yearbooks and materials
Box 6—Scrapbooks
Box 7—Old pictures
Box 8—Snow clothes
Box 9—Scrap fabrics

NOTE: I reserve boxes 15a, 15b, 15c, 15d, etc., for my income tax materials to coordinate with April 15, the IRS filing deadline. I also reserve boxes 25a, 25b, 25c, 25d, etc., for all my Christmas materials to go along with December 25.

C. File box with file folders—label as follows:

1. Report cards
2. Appliance instructions
3. Warranties
4. Decorating ideas
5. Insurance papers
6. Special notes, letters, cards
7. Car repair receipts
8. Receipts from purchases such as furniture/ antiques

NOTE: I put these file folders in my metal file cabinet or use a "Perfect Box."

Remember: "In 15 minutes a day you can be on your way to having more hours in your day."

HELPFUL HINTS

- Many household chores can be done during "in-between times"—in between outings, appointments, or TV programs. Once you realize that it takes only 15 minutes to change the sheets, you can fit this and similar tasks into the available time slots.

- The busy person's greatest need is for "effective," not "efficient" planning. Being effective means choosing the right task from all the alternatives. Being efficient means doing any job that happens to be around. The importance of planning is that it saves you time in the end. Know what you have to do and have your priorities established.

- Get rid of extra paper. Almost 90 percent of the paper in your home or office is never referred to again. Get rid of as much of it as possible.

- I find that if I break a project into a lot of small jobs and complete the little pieces, I get the job done faster. At times I even reward myself with a treat for doing a good job.

- Studies show that the success rate for people who write down their goals is about 90 times greater that of those who don't.

- You must be positive in your approach to organization. Make a list; eliminate what you don't need. Set a schedule; eliminate interruptions. Be positive about being organized. Remember, you are in charge. Total organization doesn't exist. Organization is a lifetime process. You are capable of handling your flow of appointments, clothes, money, and so forth.

- In budgeting my time on my daily calendar, I leave a cushion of 15 minutes here and there on my schedule. This way I don't find myself running from one appointment to another.

- Make a list on paper of ten goals that you wish to attain by the end of the year and do them.

15

Cleaning—It Only Takes a Minute

*There is a time for everything,
and a season for
every activity under heaven.*

Ecclesiastes 3:1, NIV

&. —— &.

Getting Started

Concentrate on how good it's going to look when you're finished cleaning the area. It's amazing how much order and organization comes about because we have cleaned. The rest of the home functions much better when we give priority to an organized and clean home.

Here's how to get going:

1. *Decide as a family how clean your home needs to be.* Each family will differ in this area. Some people require more cleanliness than others. I saw a cross-stitch picture not long ago in an antique store that said, "I need my home to be as clean to be healthy and as messy as to make it warm." That's pretty good wisdom. Remember:A home is to be lived in and not to be a sterile environment.

2. *Start early.* Don't procrastinate. Your sleeves should be rolled up and in the swing by at least 9:00 A.M.

3. *Start with something that's easy and that you like.* Is there one area or one thing that gives you satisfaction

when it's clean? For some it might be an oven, for some it might be a refrigerator, for others it might be a sparkling-clean shelf of formal china.

4. *Get several chores going at one time.* Turn on the radio to soft music, put a load of dishes in the dishwasher, do a load of wash, and start a thorough vacuum cleaning. Now you are flying. The momentum is getting the blood flowing through your veins. You become so excited you want to tell someone. However, stay off the phone—you need to focus on what you're doing.

5. *Have a good set of cleaning tools on hand.* See my "Speed Cleaning" chapters in *Things Happen When Women Care* and *The 15-Minute Organizer*. First-class tools make you feel first-class. Old tools make you discouraged, and you feel like you're doing a poor job.

6. *Decide what you're going to do beforehand.* Each evening before ending the day I jot down on my "To Do" list what needs to be done tomorrow. It helps me get started the next day. I don't have to waste time deciding "What do I do now?" Procrastinators love "To Do" lists because they provide a starting point. When you get finished with each item, be sure to check it off. It will give you a great feeling to complete each task.

7. *Promise yourself that quitting time is _____, and keep the promise. The 15-Minute Organizer* can be a big help in giving additional hints.

8. *Make big tasks into smaller tasks.* Many times the whole is too big for us to attack. However, a smaller part of the whole is manageable. For example, cleaning the whole refrigerator might be too big, but cleaning the bottom shelf on Monday, the middle shelf on Tuesday, the fruit and vegetable drawers on Wednesday, and the exterior on Thursday is doable. I call these small parts "instant tasks." Don't look at the whole—it gets overwhelming. *Think small!*

9. *On your mark, get set, go!*

Additional Ideas While Cleaning

10. *Take care of everything you have.* We forget that much of what we throw out is waste through neglect. Keep your belongings clean and repaired; this will greatly increase their life.

11. *Do it now.* Don't wait to clean up that spill, spot, or soil. Do it while it's fresh on your mind. The longer we wait to clean, the more irritated we become.

12. *Train the family to clean up after themselves.* By not doing this, they increase Mom's job. If each of them would take care of their own messes, they would learn some very valuable lessons regarding *responsibility.* Teach your family to save Mom—she is a very valuable resource.

13. *Make our homes and offices "no smoking" areas.* It's amazing how much smoking increases our cleaning cost and time.

14. *Go to your local janitorial supply houses and buy concentrates.* Why pay for water when you already have it at home? Another side benefit is that you won't have a lot of small containers going into the trash and filling up our landfills faster.

16

Using the Right Cleanser

Create in me a clean heart, O God,
and renew a steadfast spirit within me.

Psalm 51:10, NASB

ॐ ——— ॐ

Having the right tool makes any job easier. Many women call me recommending a certain product to take out a stain, spot, or soil on a fabric. I so appreciate this information.

All household cleaning products come with specific directions on the label. Read and follow them, and use the product only for recommended surfaces. You should note if any warnings are on the label.

PRODUCTS

Abrasive Cleansers

Powder — For baked-on food residue, cooking utensils, tough stains on sinks and tubs. Wet surface, apply cleanser, rub/scour as needed, and rinse.

Liquid — For ceramic bathtubs, sinks, toilet bowls. Apply to surface, rub gently, and rinse.

Air, Carpet, and Room Refreshers and Deodorizers

For counteracting odors in carpets, rooms, rugs, and upholstery. Sprinkle powdered carpet freshener on and leave ten to fifteen minutes, then vacuum. For other forms, follow package directions.

All-Purpose Cleaners

Powder and liquid

For appliance surfaces, glass, ceramic, and porcelain enamel tops/cook tops, chrome countertops, painted walls, painted and stainless steel, small plastic appliances, resilient and masonry floors, tile, window blinds/washable shades, painted woodwork. Mix with water or use liquid full strength according to package directions. Generally no rinsing is required, except for no-wax floors.

Spray

For appliances (surface and trim); chrome fixtures; countertops; small washable areas; smudges on painted walls, woodwork, doors, and around switch plates. Spray on surface. Sponge or wipe clean; dry with towel or cloth.

Ammonia*

For mirrors, glass, chrome fixtures, manually cleaned ovens, painted

---

* Do not mix chlorine bleach with vinegar, ammonia, or a toilet bowl cleaner. Toxic fumes may cause illness.

walls, stainless steel, windows, painted woodwork. *Note:* Do not use to clean plastic windows or aluminum storm-door windows. Clouding and pitting can occur. You can control the cleaning strength by increasing the ammonia from one half cup to one cup per gallon of water (depending upon the difficulty of the job). *For spray-bottle use:* Mix 1 part ammonia to 16 parts water. For windows, mirrors, and glass, use one tablespoon ammonia per one quart of water. *Note:* Use in a well-ventilated area.

Baking Soda

For removing odor from utensils, chopping boards, coffeepots, baked-on food, freezers, and refrigerators. Also use on bathtubs, sinks, shower, chrome fixtures, fiberglass, shower stalls, plastic laminates, and stains on plastic utensils, dishes, and vacuum bottles. *Dry:* Sprinkle straight from the box. Rub with a damp sponge or cloth; rinse and dry. *Solution:* Mix four tablespoons baking soda per one quart water. *Paste:* Mix three parts baking soda to one part water.

Carpet Cleaners (liquid, foam, powder)

For rugs and carpets (spots and general cleaning). Follow package directions. Some can be applied by hand; others require equipment.

Chlorine Bleach*

For disinfecting cutting boards; mildew on grout and ceramic tile, patio bricks; stains on hard surfaces, toilet bowls. Mix three-fourths cup bleach to one gallon water. Increase strength as needed.

Drain Cleaners (liquid and granular)

For dissolving grease, hair, soap-scum buildup, sluggish drains—kitchen and bathroom. Follow package directions precisely.

Dusting Products (aerosol and pump, liquid, and paste)

For furniture. Apply product to cloth, wipe over surface, buff to shine.

Glass Cleaners (liquid and spray)

For chrome, mirrors, windows, doors, and glass tabletops. *Note:* Do not use on acrylic plastic doors, windows, or clock face protectors. Spray directly on windows or on cloth or sponge for mirror or picture glass. Wipe dry.

Metal Cleaner/Polish

For brass, copper, silver, etc. Some contain an antioxidant to protect cleaned surface from rapid retarnishing. Follow package directions.

---

* Do not mix chlorine bleach with vinegar, ammonia, or a toilet bowl cleaner. Toxic fumes may cause illness.

Mildew Removers

For ceramic tile grout in showers, bathrooms. Follow package directions. *Note:* Use in well-ventilated areas. Avoid contact with fabrics.

Oven Cleaners (liquid, sponge, spray)

For removing burned fats and food deposits from ovens and barbecue grills. Follow package directions. *Note:* Use gloves while working with this product.

Pumice Stones

For toilet bowls, urinals, sinks and showers, concrete, masonry, and iron. Use plenty of water with back-and-forth motion. *Note:* Do not use on highly polished metals, glass, fiberglass, and unbaked enamel surfaces.

Scouring Pads (soap-impregnated)

For baked-on food, barbecue grills, broilers, cooking utensils, ovens. Wet and use.

Toilet Bowl Cleaners (crystal, liquid, in-tank)*

For cleaning; some also disinfect. Follow package directions.

---

* Do not mix chlorine bleach with vinegar, ammonia, or a toilet bowl cleaner. Toxic fumes may cause illness.

Tub, Tile, and Sink Cleaners (liquid and spray)

For ceramic walls; tiles; shower stalls; sinks; toilet bowl exteriors; fiberglass, plastic, and porcelain bathtubs. Apply to surface, rub gently, rinse thoroughly, and wipe dry with cloth.

Upholstery Cleaners (liquid, aerosol sprays, powder)

For upholstery fabric. Follow package directions. Test a hidden spot on the fabric.

Vinegar (white)*

For hard-water deposits on bathtubs, shower stalls/curtains, automatic drip coffeemakers, appliance exteriors, chrome, glass windows and doors, and mirrors. Use full strength or diluted, depending on use. To clean coffeemaker, fill water holder with vinegar and water and run through a brew cycle. Follow with a cycle of clear water to rinse.

---

* Do not mix chlorine bleach with vinegar, ammonia, or a toilet bowl cleaner. Toxic fumes may cause illness.

17

Setting Up a Desk and Work Area

Commit your work to the Lord,
then it will succeed.

Proverbs 16:3

ક૾ ——— ક૾

As I began to get my home in order and to eliminate all the clutter, I soon realized that I didn't have an area to handle all the mail and paper that came into our home. We have had several mottos to help us focus on our home organization. One was "Don't put it down, put it away."

Much of our clutter was little piles of materials that needed to be put away, but we just temporarily put them down until we could put them where they belonged. At the end of the day we had piles sitting all around the home. Now we take items back to where we found them. It's amazing how the piles have disappeared.

Another motto was "Don't pile it, file it." In the corners of our home we had piles of paper stacked in no organized fashion. In our new program we have taken manila folders and given them one-word headings like: *Insurance, Car, Home, Foods, Patio, Children, Utilities, Taxes.* Now we file, not pile, our papers.

During all this change in our home, we still had no central desk or work area. Yet we had identified we needed one in order to function properly with maximum effectiveness.

Paper handling depends upon a good physical setup in a practical location furnished with a comfortable working surface and a good inventory of supplies. Ideally, this office will become a permanent fixture where the business procedures of your home are done. The area should have access to supplies and files, and located where other household operations do not interfere. However, if your desk/work area can't be this ideal, don't let it stop you from getting started. Yours might have to be portable, but that's okay. Just get started.

Since a desk or work area is so basic to a smoothly functioning lifestyle, we will give you some practical steps in setting up this area in your home.

Choosing the Location

The selection of your office location depends upon how long you will spend in your office daily. If you have a business inside your home, you need to use different criteria in selecting that special site over the person who needs a place to open mail, answer mail, pay bills, and file papers. Regardless of which your need is, you want to choose a location that agrees with your spirit. If after a short while you find you aren't using your new space, but instead find yourself working in the room with a big window, you might have initially selected the wrong location. Make sure it meets your needs. It's not always practical to be located in the ideal location. We often find that there needs to be a compromise. In order to help you choose that ideal setting, you might ask yourself these questions:

• Do you need to be in a place where it's quiet, or is it better for you to be near people?

- Do big windows distract you, or do you like being near windows?
- Do you prefer a sunny room or a shaded one?
- Do you prefer to work in the morning or in the afternoon?

These last two questions are related because different rooms receive varying amounts of light at different times of the day.

The answer to these questions helps narrow your alternatives. Walk around your home to see which areas meet the answers to your four questions. After selecting at least two locations, you might ask yourself another set of questions:

- Is there enough space for your computer?
- Are there enough electrical outlets and telephone jacks?
- Is there enough space for a desk?
- Is this location out of the way of other household functions? If not, can they be shifted so they won't interfere with your office hours?
- Is the area structurally sound?

Again, add the answers to these questions to your previously selected alternatives and narrow them down to a final selection. Do you feel good about this selection? Live with it a few days before making a final selection. Walk to and through it several times to see that it feels good. Sit down in the area and read a magazine or book. If it still feels good, then you will probably like your choice.

Don't begin tearing out walls, adding electrical outlets, moving phone jacks, and building bookcases until you are sure you have found the right location.

Selection of Desk,
Equipment, and Supplies

After you have selected the location for your office, you need to take a sheet of paper and make a diagram of the floor plan with the dimensions listed. You will use this information when you want to make or select furniture for your new work area.

The Desk

In actuality, all someone really needs is a writing surface. In some cases a portable piece of plywood is all you have or need. Look around—you already may have around your home a suitable desk or table which would fit into the dimensions of the work area.

If you find a table, it should be sturdy, high enough to write at comfortably, and large enough to hold various implements on its surface.

If you can't find a desk or table in your home, buy a desk. It is an investment you won't regret. Check your local classified ads to find a bargain. One good source is in the Yellow Pages of your phone book under "Office Furniture—Used." You need not pay full price. Many times these stores will deliver to your home free or with a minimum charge.

You should have no trouble finding a desk which has the practical characteristics of office models, but is still attractive in your home. Here are a few specifications to keep in mind.

1. *Writing surface:* Your desk should be sturdy and comfortable to use, with a surface that doesn't wobble.

2. *Place for supplies:* Have at least one large drawer in which paper and envelopes can be kept in folders. If you find a desk with large drawers on each side, so much the better. There needs to be a shallow drawer with compartments for paper clips, rubber bands, and other supplies

At your local stationery store you can purchase small trays with dividers that can store these small items.

3. *Files and records:* A home office seldom has need for more than one file drawer, or sometimes two. If your desk has at least one drawer big enough to contain letter-size file folders (legal-size is preferable), all your files will probably be comfortably accommodated. If you can't purchase a file cabinet at this time, go back and read chapter 14—"Total Mess to Total Rest"—where I talk about "Perfect Boxes." These make excellent file boxes until you are able to purchase a file cabinet. Watch your newspaper for stationery "sale" offerings.

4. *Typing platform:* If you have a typewriter or a personal computer and plan to use it in your work area, try to get a desk with a built-in platform for these to rest on. If you have enough room in your office, you might want to designate a separate area in your office for typing and computer work.

If you don't have enough space for a regular stationary desk in your home, look into portable storage to house your stationery and supplies. Go again to your local office supply store and have them recommend products that will service this need. You will still need a file cabinet or its short-term substitute (the Perfect Box) and a sturdy swivel chair just for the office area. The swivel chair permits you to turn from one position to another without getting up.

Other Storage Ideas

- Wall organizers are helpful for pads, pens, calendars, and other supplies.

- Paper, pencils, and supplies can be kept in stackable plastic or vinyl storage cubes under the desk.

- Use an extra bookcase shelf to store a portable typewriter, basket of supplies, or some files.

- Decorative objects such as a ceramic mug look attractive holding pencils and pens.

- Use stackable plastic bins that can be added to for your expanded needs. Use the small style for stationery and papers, and a larger size (a vegetable bin) for magazines and newspapers.

Supplies

For your shopping convenience I have given you a checklist of supplies that you will need to stock your office. Try to purchase these items on sale or at an office supply discount store. Watch your local paper for these sales. "Let the Yellow Pages do the walking for you." Look under "Office Supplies." Many times bulk buying is where you will get your best prices.

- Address book or Rolodex—I personally like both. The address book I take with me when traveling or on business, and I keep a Rolodex permanently housed on my desk. The Rolodex also has more room for adding other information you might want to use when addressing that particular person/business.

- Appointment calendar—Ideally the calendar should be small enough to carry around with your notebook, as well as for use at your desk. If you search around, you can find a combination notebook and calendar that isn't too bulky to carry around in your briefcase or handbag. The date squares should be large enough to list appointments comfortably. In our Working Woman's Seminars we offer two excellent organizers called the

Harper House Day Runner and the Busy Woman's Daily Planner (devotional edition). These products do an excellent job of meeting this need.

- Bulletin board—This is a good place to collect notes and reminders to yourself. Attach notes with pushpins.

- Business cards—a must time-saver.

- Carbon paper—Make a carbon copy of every business letter your write. Your office supply store can help you with this selection. Every year new types come on the market.

- Desk lamp—A three-way bulb will give you a choice of light.

- Dictionary and/or a new calculator speller.

- File folders—I use colored "third-cut" folders in which the stick-up tabs are staggered so they don't block each other from view. The colors give a more attractive appearance to your file drawer.

- Letter opener.

- Marking pens—It is useful to have on hand a few marking pens in different colors. I do a lot of color-coding on my calendar. I also use a yellow "hi-lite" pen when I want some information to pop out at me for rereading. (See my chapter on "Paper, What to Do with All the Paper" in *Survival for Busy Women* [Harvest House Publishers].)

- Paper clips—regular and large.

- Postcards—save money on your mailing.

- Pencil sharpener—If you use a lot of pencils, I recommend the desktop electric model.

- Pencils and pens.

- Postage scale—a small, inexpensive type.

- Rubber bands—mixed sizes.

- Rubber stamp and ink pad—There are all kinds of rubber stamps that you can use in your office. These are much cheaper than printed stationery or labels. If you use a certain one over and over, you might consider having a self-inking stamp made for you—it's a great time-saver.

- Ruler.

- Scissors.

- Scratch paper—Use lined pads for this. 3-M "Post-It Notes" are also great.

- Scotch tape and dispenser.

- Stamps—In addition to regular stamps, keep appropriate postage on hand for additional weight and special handling if you do these types of mailings regularly. Postcards will save you money on certain types of correspondence.

- Stapler, staples, staple remover—If you do a lot of stapling, you might consider an electric model. It saves time and the palms of your hands.

- Stationery and envelopes—Usually the 8½" x 11" plain white paper with matching business-size envelopes is all you will need. If you use printed letterhead stationery, you will need to get some plain white or matching colored second sheets. I find 9" x 6" and 9" x 12" manila envelopes are good for mailing bulk documents, books, or magazines. Sometimes a #6 Jiffy padded envelope is useful to ship items that need some protection from rough handling in transit.

- Telephone—An extension right at your desk is great. I use my cordless telephone for this, and it works just fine. It's not as good as a permanent phone, but it's a good alternative.

- Typewriter—if you have the skills.

- Typewriter correction paper or "Liquid Paper."

- Wastebasket.

You now have an office space that can function to meet your maximum needs. This addition to your lifestyle should certainly make you more efficient in other areas of your life. It will give you a feeling of accomplishment.

18

Record-Keeping Made Simple

If you are untrustworthy about worldly wealth, who will trust you with the true riches of heaven?

Luke 16:11

𝕫𝕒 —— 𝕫𝕒

This is the year to get our records, bills, and receipts out of shoeboxes, closets, drawers, and old envelopes. I found that I could clean out my wardrobe closet fairly easily. An old skirt, stained blouse, or misfit jacket posed little difficulty for me to toss; however, where and when I should toss old financial records was very difficult. I didn't want to do the wrong thing, so I had started keeping everything—usually for too long.

At income-tax time my neck always got stiff because I knew Bob was going to ask for a canceled check or a paid invoice, and I wasn't sure where I had it. At that point, I made a decision to get my record-keeping in order so that it was a very easy process to keep my records up-to-date.

I sat down and looked at the whole process of record-keeping and began to break it down into logical steps. My first step was to decide to keep my records. Since I like things to be in order with the minimum amount of paperwork, I used to have a tendency to throw away records that should have been saved. I found that throwing away Bob's salary stubs, last year's tax return, and current receipts for medical or business expenses would only bring problems further down the road.

Our CPA says that throwing away financial records is the biggest mistake that people make. Throwing away records that later turn out to be important causes people a lot of unnecessary work and worry, he cautioned. When you have an IRS audit and you can't prove your deductions by a canceled check or a paid invoice, you will lose that deduction for that year, plus be subject to a fine and interest due. Records are very important.

Good financial records help you make decisions very quickly. In just a few moments you can retrieve valuable information so that a decision can be made for budget planning, future purchases, or anticipated future income.

As I began to develop a method by which to establish good record-keeping, I came up with a seven-step plan.

STEP 1: Know what to keep. I discovered that records generally fall into two categories: *permanent records* (important to keep throughout your life) and *transitory* records (dealing with your current circumstances).

Permanent records would include personal documents required in applying for credit, qualifying for a job, or proving entitlement to Social Security and other government programs. Birth and marriage certificates, Social Security cards, property records, college transcripts, diplomas, and licenses fall into this category.

Deciding how long to retain transitory records can be more difficult because often you don't know how long you'll need them. As a rule of thumb, I suggest you keep all employment records until you leave the job. Other transitory records you want to keep include receipts for any major purchases you have made—jewelry, autos, art, stock certificates, tax returns and receipts for at least three years, health insurance policies, credit union membership, and company stock ownership plans. Canceled checks not relating directly to specifics like home improvements should be kept for a minimum of three years in case of a tax audit; however, I will usually keep five to six years just to make sure I'm not throwing any records away that I might need on a tax audit.

If you own your home, apartment, or mobile home, be sure to retain the receipts for any improvements you make until you sell the property. They become proof that you added to the property's value and reduce any capital gains you might owe. Don't discard these receipts or tax returns from the year in which you paid for the improvements. I usually make a copy of these kind of receipts and keep a permanent copy in my folder labeled "HOME." I have found that this saves a lot of valuable time when I need to justify each record. In my "HOME" folder I also keep a running log with date, improvement made, cost, and receipt for each expenditure. At any given time we know how much money we have invested in our home. This information really helps when you get ready to sell your home and want to establish a selling price.

Your tax return, wage statements, and other papers supporting your income and deductions should be kept at least three years (that's the IRS statute of limitations for examining your return). I retain our records for six years, because the IRS has the right to audit within six years if they believe you omitted an item accounting for more than 25 percent of your reported income, or indefinitely if they believe you committed fraud.

STEP 2: Know yourself when you set up your system. Try to keep your system as simple as you can. I have found that the more disorganized you are, the simpler the system should be. It doesn't make sense to set up an elaborate filing system if it is too complicated for you to follow.

I suggest that you consider these points when setting up your system:

- How much time can you devote to record-keeping? The less time you have, the simpler your system should be.

- Do you like working with numbers? Are you good at math? If so, your system can be more complex.

- How familiar are you with tax deductions and financial planning? If you are a beginner, set up a simple system.

- Will anyone else be contributing records to the system?

This last point is a very important consideration if you are married. Usually our mate will have a different opinion on what type of system we should have. I have found among married couples that it is best to determine who is most gifted in this area and let that person take care of the records. Bob and I get along very well in this area. I write the checks for our home expenses and balance this checking account statement. Then I forward the statement to Bob for record-keeping. In our family he is the most gifted in this area.

We have found that the simplest way to organize receipts for tax purposes is to keep two file folders: one for deduction items, and another for questionable items. At tax time all you have to do is total up each category and fill in the blank. Be sure to double-check for overlooked possibilities.

If your return is more complex, set up a system with individual folders for the various deductions you claim:

medical and dental expenses, business, travel and entertainment, property taxes, interest on loans, and child-care services. When you pay a bill, drop the receipt into the right folder. At the end of the year, you'll be able to tally the receipts and be set to enter the totals on your tax forms.

Be sure to take your questionable deduction folder with you when you go to see your CPA. Go over each item to see if it is eligible for a deduction. As you can tell by reading this chapter, I strongly endorse using a professional tax preparer. Our tax returns have become difficult and the tax laws so complex that good stewardship of your monies is to go to a professional. This person will save you much more than you will spend for his or her services.

Your checkbook can be your best record-keeper if you check off entries that might count as tax deductions. If you have a personal computer at home, there is a wide selection of software programs to help you keep track of these records.

STEP 3: Set aside a spot for your records. Generally, your home rather than the office is the best place for personal documents. A fireproof, waterproof file cabinet or desk drawer will do for transitory records. However, I use and have thousands of other ladies all across the United States using our "Perfect Boxes" for storage of records. See my chapter on "Total Mess to Total Rest" for more details regarding the use of these boxes.

Permanent documents generally should be kept in a safe-deposit box. However, a will and important final instructions should be kept elsewhere because, in many states, safe-deposit boxes are sealed following the owner's death, even if someone else has a key.

STEP 4: Tell someone where your records are. As I travel around the country conducting seminars, many of the ladies share with me that they don't know where their husbands have anything written down, such as who to contact in case of their death. None of us think about death because it seems so far away, but we must share this important information with someone who will need to know.

Each year Bob reviews with me his "data sheet" listing all the information regarding insurance policies, stock and investments, mortgage locations, banking account information, contents in safe-deposit boxes, etc. That information is very helpful and reassuring to me in case of any changes in our status.

Even if you're a whiz at keeping financial records, it's not much use if no one else knows where any of your records are located. As a family, make up a list noting where your records are located and give it to a family member or trusted friend.

STEP 5: Get professional advice on handling records. As I've shared previously in this chapter, Bob and I recommend that you seek professional advice on how better records can translate into tax savings in the future. The expense is well worth the investment of time and money. You can also go to your local bookstore and purchase any number of good paperback books on this topic. Be a reader and a learner. It will serve you well.

STEP 6: Change your record-keeping system when you make a life change. Major life shifts—a job move, marriage, death, divorce, separation—signal a time to revamp your records. Starting a home-based business also means it's time to talk to the professional regarding new tax allowances. A life change does necessitate a change in record-keeping.

The costs of looking for a new job in the same field and a job-related move can mean you're eligible for a new tax deduction, so be sure to file all receipts.

STEP 7: Set aside time for your record-keeping. Try to set a regular time each month to go over your financial records so that you won't be a wreck come April when you have to file your tax return. The best system in the world won't work if you don't use it or keep it current.

Many people prefer to update records when they pay bills. Others file receipts, update a ledger of expenses, and look over permanent records once a month when reconciling a checking account. Doing whatever works best for you is what's important. You should update at least once a month. If not, you will create a lot of stress to play catch-up. The advantage of simple record-keeping is to reduce stress in our lives, not to increase the stress.

I have found that time is worth money. When I can save time, I can increase money, because my energy is better spent on constructive efforts rather than on always dealing with emergencies and putting out fires.

19

Kitchen Organization

*Those who are peacemakers will plant
seeds of peace and reap
a harvest of goodness.*

James 3:18

ક્ષ —— ક્ષ

Do you realize that one of the reasons you're crying for kitchen organization is because you spend an average of 1092 hours a year in the kitchen? That's a lot of hours in an area that definitely needs to be organized.

What You'll Need

First you'll need some jars. You can start by collecting mayonnaise jars. Those little marinated artichoke jars are also great to store things in. Tupperware is a wonderful thing to have as well. If you don't have it, maybe you need to get invited to a Tupperware party and start getting some Tupperware pieces that you can use. Those lazy Susan turntables are also super.

Also get contact paper, newspapers, or anything that you can cover some boxes with. You'll also need trash bags, plus a felt-tip marker pen and some labels.

Scheduling Time

The next crucial thing is to schedule a time. Here's what I recommend: Set the timer on your stove for 15 minutes, then work like mad until the timer goes off. Then do whatever else you have to. If you're working toward a deadline, you have a tendency to move a little faster. So schedule yourself a time in the day when you're going to organize your kitchen.

Proverbs 16:3 says that we are to commit our works to the Lord, and then they will succeed. If we are in a position to make a commitment to organizing our kitchen, we need to pray about it. God is interested in the very tiny things about us, even getting the cupboards cleaned in the kitchen. Commit your works to Him. Ask Him to give you the time and enthusiasm you need to put this into practice.

In the Kitchen

Now we're in the kitchen. First let's get some of our cupboard doors open. We don't want to open every single one of them because we'll be knocking our heads and passing out, but we need to start with, let's say, the upper cupboards. So we open all those up and start pulling everything out, starting with the cupboards closest to the sink (because these are the ones we get in and out of the most and that are probably in the biggest mess). We'll want to take everything out, get all the shelves wiped out, and then repaper them, perhaps using contact paper. Maybe we'll also want to repaint the shelves.

Now for the things you're not using. You know you have things in your kitchen that you've been storing for a long time but haven't been using, such as broken dishes, mugs, and vases, plus cleansers and other things that are partially used but you'll never use again. Put these in either your Throw Away bag or your Give Away bag, or else in a box that you use as a kitchen overflow container. (Mark some of your boxes "Kitchen Overflow." You may need several of these.) These seldom-used boxes can be stored on the garage shelves where you have extra room.

Next you have items that you use daily. For these buy a turntable that is made specifically for using underneath your kitchen sink. You can put all your cleansers and so forth on this handy item.

Equipment Priorities

Priority use means that those things which you use all the time will go back into the cupboards. Such things as spices, dishes, pots and pans, etc., should be put back neatly. I use lazy Susan turntables for my spices. I don't think you can have enough turntables. Or you can use a spice rack. (A spice rack also comes in handy for vitamin bottles.)

The things you don't use very often should go back in the cupboards, on the highest shelves. This might include such things as big platters for your Thanksgiving turkey. (You might use this only once or twice a year.)

Then get your broken appliances repaired. They're sitting around waiting for somebody to pay attention to them. Those with a cost to repair more than half the cost of a new appliance should be thrown out.

For those of you who have high school students going into college, save your appliances that are a little old-fashioned or just extra. Put them in a box and store them away. We found that when our children went off to college they started getting their own apartments, and they wanted such things as the extra iron, toaster, etc. So start saving these things for them. Put them in a box, label them, and number them. Then put this information in your card files.

Kitchen Overflow

Now for your overflow: At one time Bob and I and the children lived in a condominium. We had moved from a big two-story house to a small three-bedroom condo-minium. I found that when I was organizing the kitchen I didn't have a place for everything. That's when I discov-ered what I call the kitchen overflow. It you're lucky enough to have a shelf or cabinets in the garage, that's a good place to put the overflow. If not, get some boxes with lids and put the overflow in them. The overflow might include such things as a waffle iron, an extra set of dishes, or even extra canned goods.

Many of you may be living in apartments, mobile homes, or other smaller quarters where you don't have a lot of cupboard space. This has been one of the frequent complaints that I've heard from women: "What do I do with all this stuff? I don't have enough room for it." Well, when the overflow is in uniform boxes, it can go in a bedroom or closet or out in the garage somewhere.

What should you do with gadgets and utensils if you're short on space? Put them in a crock and tie a little bow around it. The crock looks cute on the counter, and all your whips and wooden spoons and spatulas can probably fit in it. Set the crock close to the stove or at some other handy spot.

Unavoidable Junk

Then there are the junk drawers. There is no way to eliminate these, so don't feel you have to get rid of those junk drawers. We all have them. The problem is, they are usually very junky. So we can take that junk and pretty well clean it up. My junk drawer has a little silverware sectional container. It comes in all colors. In it I put the hammer, the screwdriver, and a couple of those small artichoke jars in which I keep some cup hooks, nails, screws, and thumbtacks—all those little things. You may want to get two or three jars to put in your junk drawer so you'll have everything fairly organized when you pull it out. (The reason why jars are nice is because you can see what's inside them.)

Another handy organizer is an egg carton. This is fabulous to use for those little screws. You can cut apart the cartons so that you have small sections of egg cartons. Then the screws, hooks, etc., can fit in there and go nicely in your junk drawer. Another neat thing to do with an egg carton is to open it up and put it in the bottom of the paper bag you use as a garbage can liner. It absorbs the moisture and takes care of all the gunky stuff that falls to the bottom. Then when the children take out the bag, it won't fall apart and drip all over the kitchen.

I've found that it's not really what you do that makes you tired, but what you don't do. The mental pressure that we have about all those things we need to do makes us worry and become concerned, and we get tired over it. So we need to get moving and do the job.

Pantry Space

You're lucky if you have a pantry. If you don't have a pantry, you may have a cupboard in your kitchen that you're using as a pantry. Not many of us are fortunate enough to have a walk-in pantry like Grandma used to have, where she could put all her bowls and flour and sugar. I've opened women's pantries not to see what's there, but just to get something out for someone, and I've found all kinds of toys, books, etc., that should be in other parts of the house. If you have small children and need to keep some of their things in the pantry, then get something like a plastic laundry basket to keep all their toys in.

Potatoes or onions can be kept in colored plastic stack trays. These trays are also wonderful to use in closets in your bedrooms, particularly for your children.

Making the Pantry Cute

The pantry can be organized in a really fun and cute way. You can label the shelves with one of those tape labelers. (Maybe you already have one.) I have a friend who has everything labeled in her pantry—where the soups go, where the ketchup goes, etc. Why does she do that? Because she has older children who put her groceries away when she comes in from the market. Also, she entertains a lot, and various people put things back in the pantry. I have another friend whose husband has taken wooden dowels and fastened them along the shelf of the pantry so that the canned goods slide in. That's real organization!

For packaged items, such as dried taco mix, salad dressings, gravies, etc., get a shoebox and cover it with the wallpaper from your kitchen or extra wallpaper that you have or contact paper, and it will look cute in the pantry. You can also purchase plastic or metal sliding shelves. They're not as inexpensive as the other things I've mentioned, but they make for a neat pantry.

Put everything you can in jars. (You might go to a fast-food store and ask for some of those big mustard and mayonnaise jars.) My jars in the pantry have everything in them—rice, Bisquick, popcorn, beans, sugar, flour, graham crackers, cookies, raisins, coffee filters, dog biscuits—everything.

We had a problem because the mice liked the dog biscuits out in the garage, and I was finding mouse droppings around. So I took a big jar and put the dog biscuits in it. This way we got rid of the mice, and the biscuits look real cute in the jar!

Work Together, Store Together

Things that work together should be stored together. What does that mean? If you're going to organize baking items—your mixing bowls, your hand mixer, your measuring cups—all those things can be stored in one small area together. I bake homemade bread, so I have on my shelf all those things that I use to bake the bread. I have my pans, the oil, the honey, the flour, the yeast, etc., handy, so that when I'm ready to bake bread I don't have to be running from cupboard to cupboard trying to find things. After I bake the bread I put everything back on the shelf. Once things in your kitchen have a place, then they should go back to that place. Once they find their place and your family members get used to it, they will begin to put things back in their areas.

Knives and Pans

Get your knives sharpened, because you have a problem when you pick up a knife that's dull. If you never use a particular knife, throw it out.

Pots and pans should be kept neatly somewhere near the stove. You can line the shelves for the pots with plain or light-colored paper—maybe brown paper. I bought some rubber pads to keep my frying pans and other heavy potware from scratching and ruining my shelf lining. Determine the best possible position for your pans, because those are things you use often and need to get out quickly. You can draw a circle or square the size of the pan with a black felt pen, then write the pan size inside the circle or square. For example, here is where the nine-inch frying pan goes and that's where the two-quart saucepan goes. If you have people other than yourself doing things in your kitchen, this is a wonderful way for them to know where things are to be stored.

The Refrigerator

What about the refrigerator? If you're working through your card file, you'll remember that a refrigerator only needs to be cleaned once a month. So the first week of every month you're going to clean your refrigerator. (You have one whole week to do it.) Look at that refrigerator as just another closet, because basically that's what it is—a cold-storage closet.

Your vegetables can be put in your Tupperware or plastic containers or baggies. The cheese and meats go on the coldest shelf. Put them in see-through containers also. You can even put some of these things in jars if you like. And remember to rotate your eggs.

Lazy Susans are great space-savers in your refrigerator. I have two of them. One is on the top shelf and stores the milk and the half-and-half. The other one has the sour cream, the cottage cheese, etc.

You can also buy dispensers and bottle racks for your refrigerator. Can dispensers are good if you use a lot of soft drinks. Some dispensers you can set right onto the shelf in your refrigerator, and they dispense from right there. There are also special milk dispensers, juice dispensers, and so forth. Your children will absolutely love these. So if you buy a dispenser for the first time, put something really healthful in it, such as milk or orange juice, because they'll love to get a drink just to use the dispenser.

The Freezer

Now what about the freezer? When I go to the market and come home with hamburger meat, I prepare that meat to put into the freezer. I make patties, stick them on a cookie sheet, and put them right into the freezer. They'll freeze in an hour or two. Then, as soon as they're frozen, I take them out and put them in either a baggie or a plastic container, so that when I'm ready a week later to get the hamburger out of the freezer, the patties don't stick together. This way I can bring out two hamburger patties or ten. If I'm going to make meat loaf, I just take out five or six hamburger patties and make them into meat loaf.

Keep ahead of your ice cubes, especially if it's summertime and you don't have an icemaker. Bag up some ice cubes and put them in the freezer so you'll have extras when you need them.

All your frozen vegetables should be put in one section and your meats in another section. All your casseroles that you premake can also be put together. When I make a lasagna casserole or spaghetti sauce, I make enough for that night plus one for the freezer. And I always label and date containers so I'll know how long they've been in the freezer.

I also try to keep emergency meals in the freezer in case company drops in or I've been too busy to prepare anything else. You can buy plastic containers especially for making TV dinners. With these, if you have leftovers from the meal, you can put together one TV dinner with foil around the top, then label it and put it into the freezer. When you get four or five of these accumulated, you've got a nice meal for everyone that's just a little different.

Be sure you label dishes that go into the freezer, because otherwise you'll find mystery packages in the freezer as you clean it out. It's amazing how things change when they're frozen! They don't look the same!

Ice cream and frozen desserts should go together in your freezer. Did you know that you can freeze potato chips, corn chips, tortillas, muffins, and bread? If you use wheat flour, be sure to keep that in the freezer so it will keep nice and fresh. Candles should also be kept in the freezer, particularly if you've bought them at a discount price. (If you keep them in the freezer, they won't drip or pop when you light them.)

This and That

Let's talk about some miscellaneous items. Kitchen towels and cloths should be kept in a drawer or on a shelf that's close at hand, and pot holders near the point of use. Anytime you put something on a rack, it will be a space-saver for you. Plastic racks come in all sizes and are very inexpensive. For example, your dishes can go on place-holders especially designed for that purpose.

I keep a lazy Susan under every bathroom sink in the house. The shampoos and hair sprays can go on a lazy Susan. The cleaning products can go in a little basket or bucket. This way everything is right there in one container that you can pick up and take with you when you're cleaning throughout the house.

Keep a coffee can full of baking soda near the stove in case of a grease fire, and label the can with a felt-tip pen. Be sure to teach your children what the baking soda is for and how to use it.

Always load your sharp knives in the dishwasher with the blades down. Teach your children to do this also, so they don't cut themselves. All of us have cut ourselves at one time or another on a freshly sharpened knife, so we need to be careful with cutlery. Don't cook over an open flame in billowing, long sleeves. Don't, for example, go into the kitchen in your negligee and start cooking over the open flame. Be sure to roll up your sleeves.

Joyful in the Process

First Thessalonians 5:16-18 says, "Always be joyful. Always keep on praying. No matter what happens, always be thankful, for this is God's will for you who belong to Christ Jesus." We sometimes become overwhelmed with our homes as we struggle from "total mess to total rest." Some of you haven't gotten it done. But that's okay as long as you're in the process. This is particularly true of your kitchen. You've got a lot of things to organize, and maybe not a lot of room in which to do it, but don't let it become overwhelming.

God says that we are to be joyful in our homes and around our husbands. So we need to keep on praying no matter what happens. Sometimes we don't feel like having an attitude of prayer in our homes, and that's when we need to ask God to give us that joyful attitude no matter what happens. We need to continue with an attitude of prayer as we organize our kitchen.

Another wonderful thing to do is to turn on some good music. If you have any good Christian tapes or good Christian radio stations, turn them on and allow God to speak to you through His music as you organize your home.

You spend a lot of time in your home, so make it a joyful place. Pray about your attitude toward your kitchen and your meals and the presentation of those meals to your family. Then let the music flow in your heart because of the love of our Lord, Jesus Christ.

KITCHEN ORGANIZATION SUMMARY

This is the day which the LORD has made;
let us rejoice and be glad in it.
(Psalm 118:24, NASB)

Equipment Needed

- Jars (assorted sizes)
- Tupperware—various sizes
- Rubbermaid lazy Susans and turntables
- Large "Perfect Box"—labeled "Kitchen Overflow"
- Contact paper to match the colors of your kitchen
- Trash bag marked "Throw Away"
- Felt-tip pen
- Labels

Schedule a Free Time

> *Commit your work to the Lord,*
> *then it will succeed.*
> (Proverbs 16:3)

A. Open all cupboard doors.
   1. Begin with cupboard closest to sink.
   2. Take *everything* out.
   3. Wipe out shelves and repaper with contact paper if needed.
   4. Eliminate, throw away, or put aside any item that is not used daily (example: odd mugs, glasses, plastic forks, utensils). Sharpen dull knives or throw them away.

B. Prime-time equipment goes back into cupboards
   —Spices used often
   —Glasses
   —Dishes
   —Pots and pans, etc.

C. Seldom-used equipment goes to the back of cupboards or on the highest shelves.

D. Put aside broken appliances to be repaired, or get rid of them now. Look in your telephone Yellow Pages for "Appliance Repair."

Overflow

Box and store in garage: odd vases, dishes, platters, pans, camping equipment (can be put into its own marked box), canned goods, seldom-used appliances (waffle iron, juicer, blender).

Gadgets and Utensils

Put wooden spoons, ladles, long-handled spoons and forks, and potato masher into a crock or ceramic pot.

This saves space and looks very decorative on the countertop.

Junk Drawers

Get plastic dividers (usually used for flatware). Use them to hold such things as a small hammer, thumbtacks, a small plastic box or small jar with nails, cup hooks, a screwdriver, pliers, tweezers, glue, flashlight batteries, fuses, matches, scissors, and other miscellaneous items. Plastic egg cartons, when cut, make great organizers.

Pantry

You're lucky if you have one. *It's for food only*—not papers, books, or toys!

A. Sort out food items.

B. Label shelf to indicate food items: soups, fruits, vegetables, cereals, salad dressings. Baking section includes flour, sugar, baking soda, mixes.

C. Packaged items such as dry taco mix, salad dressing, gravy, etc., should be put into a large jar or small shoebox covered with contact paper or wallpaper.

D. Put everything you can in jars—tea bags, plastic spoons and forks, nuts, flour, cereal, sugar, chips, croutons, beans, noodles, rice, oatmeal, popcorn, spaghetti, graham crackers, cookies, raisins, coffee filters, dog biscuits.

Things That Work Together Should Be Stored Together

A. Baking items, mixing bowls, hand mixer, measuring cups, etc.

B. Coffeepot, filters, coffee, and perhaps mugs.

Pots and Pans

A. To keep these neatly, line shelves with plain or light-colored paper.

B. Determine the best possible position for each item.

C. Draw an exaggerated outline of the item on the shelf paper with a black felt-tip pen. You can also write the pan's description within the borders of the outline.

Refrigerator

A. Look at it as just another closet.

B. Fruits and vegetables should be put into plastic containers with lids, or in plastic bags, or in refrigerator drawers.

C. Cheese and meats go on the coldest shelf (use all types of see-through containers with tight lids).

D. Eggs—remember to rotate the oldest to the front or to the right depending on whether you have a drawer or shelf for eggs.

E. Lazy Susans, a space-saver, will hold sour cream, cottage cheese, jellies, peanut butter, yogurt, and mustard. A lazy Susan on the top shelf will hold milk, half-and-half, an orange juice jar, or a bottle of cold water.

F. You can also buy can dispensers and bottle racks which attach to the refrigerator shelf.

Freezer

A. Freeze hamburger meat shaped into patties on a

cookie sheet and then transfer the meat to plastic bags. The patties won't stick together that way. (They thaw quickly for meat loaf, burger patties, tacos, casseroles, or spaghetti sauce.)

B. Keep ahead of ice cubes. Periodically bag up a bunch and store them.

C. Frozen packaged vegetables all go together.

D. Date and label all leftovers. Avoid mystery packages. Leftovers store great in Ziploc bags, or wrap them tightly with foil to avoid freezer burn.

E. Ice cream and frozen desserts go together.

F. Potato chips, corn chips, nuts, breads, muffins, wheat flour, tortillas, flour, corn, and candles (to keep them from dripping) all freeze well.

G. Make ahead: lasagna, noodle and cheese casseroles, soups, beans, spaghetti sauce, enchiladas. Be sure to date and label. Also, if you are freezing in jars, be sure to leave 1½" at the top to allow for expansion.

Miscellaneous

A. Kitchen towels and cloths
   1. Put in a drawer or on a shelf close to the sink.
   2. Keep pot holders near point of use.

B. Racks
   1. They double your dish space and cupboard space.
   2. Plastic utensil drawers can be purchased at hardware stores at low expense.
   3. They come in various sizes and will fit together.
   4. These can also be used in bathroom and bedroom drawers.

C. Cleaning products should be put in one area with dustcloths and a few rags. Include window cleaner, waxes, Comet-type cleaners.

HELPFUL HINTS

- To avoid a smelly garbage disposal, run cold water with the disposal for a while with each use.

- Use pressure cookers, microwaves, electric pans, or small electric ovens when you can. They use less energy than your stove or regular oven.

- Do not store cookies, cereal, or other "bait" by the stove. Children can get burned climbing on the stove to reach an item overhead.

- Use glass or ceramic pans for baking; you can reduce your oven temperature by 25° F.

- I've found an easy way to clean the cheese grater: Before using it, spray it with no-stick vegetable spray.

- Put a decorative hook by the sink. Hang your watch and rings on it while you work.

- Match the size of the pan to the heating element so more heat will get to the pan.

- If you have a gas stove, make sure the pilot light is burning efficiently with a blue flame. A yellowish flame needs adjustment.

- Cook with a clock or timer; don't open the oven door continually to check food.

- Glue a 12-inch square of cork to the inside of the cabinet door over your kitchen work area. On the cork tack the recipe card you are using and newspaper clippings of recipes you plan to try within a few days. It keeps them at eye level and they stay spatter-free.

- When using your electric can opener, help save your fingers from cuts by placing a refrigerator magnet on top of the can before opening it. This magnet will give you a good grip when you lift off the lid.

- Increase your efficiency with an extra-long phone cord that will reach to all corners of your kitchen. Instead of wasting time while on the phone, you can cook, set the table, or clean out a drawer. A speaker phone provides similar freedom.

- Meat slices easier if it's partially frozen.

- Want to mix frozen juice in a hurry without using the blender? Use your potato masher on the concentrate.

- You can peel garlic cloves faster if you mash them lightly with the side of the blade of a chef's knife.

- To keep bugs out of your flour canister, put a stick of spearmint gum in the flour and it will be bug-free.

20

Odds and Ends

*For I can do everything
God asks me to with
the help of Christ who gives me
the strength and power.*

Philippians 4:13

❧ —— ❧

Now we need to take care of the odds and ends throughout our home to help us be organized. Once or twice a year I go to a card shop where they have all kinds of greeting cards—birthday cards, anniversary cards, sympathy cards, etc. Rather than running out 15 or 20 times during the year, I spend 30 minutes to an hour once or twice a year at a card shop. I take the sheet labeled "Dates and Occasions" to help me pick out the cards for everyone that I'm going to need to send a card to throughout the year. Along with that I'll add some anniversary cards, get-well cards, and sympathy cards. (I need a few of those on hand.) Then I file all the cards in file folders marked "Greeting Cards."

The Gift Shelf

Somewhere in your home it's nice to have a gift shelf. At any of the department stores that have sales, pick up a few nice items. A little box of stationery, little teddy bears, or whatever is useful and on sale should go on your shelf. I've always had a gift shelf in my home. When the children had a birthday party they had to go to, I would let them go pick out what they wanted from the shelf to give to Scotty or Lori or whomever. This way you've got something right there all the time, so you're not running out to a department store spending a lot of time and money. Where it's only costing you two or three dollars this way, you might have spent ten or fifteen dollars because you were in a hurry and didn't have the time to find bargains. So have an area in your home for some toys and books and other small gift items all ready to go.

The Gift Wrap Shelf

Then I also like to have a gift wrap shelf (or box or drawer). Once a year I'll go to where they have gift wrap on sale. (We have several places in our area, and you may also.) Once a year I buy all my Christmas wrap plus dried flowers and everything I need to wrap packages. One year I had red-and-white polka-dot paper for Christmas. I didn't stop using it once Christmas was over. Anytime during the year I could put a red ribbon on that paper, or a white or blue or yellow ribbon. And I had that same wrap for any occasion throughout the year. So I always had something with which I could wrap a package right away.

In that gift-wrap section you should have some colored ribbon, Scotch tape, and a few dried or silk flowers to put on a package. Another cute thing is to go out to the yard and pick some creeping Charlie and stick it on a package (or a few chrysanthemums, daisies, or other fresh flowers). Then you should also have some brown paper for mailing packages, along with mailing labels and some strapping tape.

The Home Office

Somewhere in your home you should have a home office. This is wonderful to have, perhaps in the kitchen, a bedroom, or even the garage. In this office should be a desk, some shelves, scissors, paper clips, pens, pencils, Scotch tape, thank-you notes, marking pens, postcards, and stamps. (I hate to stand in line at the post office. Every time I go, the line seems to get longer. So I go once or twice a year. I buy a nice, big, fat roll of stamps that costs a lot of money, but I figure it's worth it because I don't have to go so often.)

Also have a glue stick, a rubber stamp pad, and a rubber stamp. When our children were about 15 years old, I put in their Christmas stockings a rubber stamp pad and a rubber stamp made with their name, address, and telephone number. They could use this on their school papers or for a return address on the cards and thank-you notes that they send out. You don't give this to a five-year-old because if you do, he'll be stamping his name all over the wallpaper and everywhere else. So use your head on this. But kids love those little rubber stamps, and they make super gifts.

Then get some stationery, a letter opener, a memo pad, a paperweight, some string, a dictionary, and a file box with your colored file folders. You already have these from your five-week program, so this is no extra trouble. (See chapter 17 for more details on having a home office.)

Telephone Items

What do you actually keep next to your telephone? One of the things I dislike is making a telephone address book. Every so many years (or months) you have to redo the address book, and I just hate that because it takes a lot of time. I found this handy telephone address file that has the separate cards that can be pulled out. One brand is called a Rolodex Card File. With this system you fill out a separate card for each person, then if there's a change you can either erase the information or fill out a new card. This way you just change the cards gradually as time goes on instead of rewriting a whole book once a year. On these cards you can list birthdays, anniversaries, clothing sizes for your family, directions to friends' homes, and other pertinent information.

By your telephone you should have some pens and pencils, some scissors, a letter opener, a memo pad, and a calling card file. A calling card file is a little packet that has plastic pages inside in which you can insert business cards. Remember that Put Away bag that now has those business cards from drawers and all over the place? Well, now you have a place to put them—in this nice little packet. This can go in a drawer by the telephone, and it makes a great gift for Father's Day. It's nice for a stocking stuffer at Christmas, too.

Also by your telephone you should have your emergency telephone numbers. (See the sheet covering this described in chapter 5.)

Your Own Business Card

You should consider the possibility of having your own business card. I know you're saying, "But I'm just a mom; I don't need a business card or calling card." My sister-in-law gave me some calling cards when our children were little. They had my name, telephone number, and then all around the card they had all the fun things that I like to do. As it turned out, I couldn't believe how much I used those cards. I'd see a mother at school who would tell me her son was going to come home with my son to play and I'd give her a card so she could have my phone number and address. Instead of fumbling through my purse finding a pen and piece of paper, all I did was zip out my business card and hand it to her. She would look at it and say, "That's neat. I didn't know you knew how to make homemade bread," or "I didn't know you taught a time management class."

Things in Your Car

Then consider the things you keep in the glove compartment or trunk of your automobile. These things will help to keep you at ease. You should have a flashlight, some maps, a can opener, change for emergency telephone calls, reading material, business cards, a few Band-Aids, matches, stationery, pens and pencils, a blanket, a towel, and scissors.

In the trunk you should have a few fuses, a rope, a fire extinguisher, jumper cables, flares, and a first-aid kit.

21

Garage Organization

*We can make our plans, but the
final outcome is in God's hands.*

Proverbs 16:1

❧ —— ❧

"Help! I'm in the garage! Over here. No,
silly, not over there—in the middle of the
garage, third heap on your left.

"Come fast! Help! I'm under the newspapers and magazines. Thank you! Look at all this mess. Can you believe it? We really do need to clean this garage."

What You'll Need

1. Trash bags

2. Jars—mayonnaise, peanut butter, and jelly size

3. Small metal cabinets with plastic drawers. You can purchase these at a hardware store to take the place of jars.

4. Large hooks—the type you hang bicycles on

5. Boxes—cardboard-type used for apples and oranges. Most supermarkets have them. Or use More Hours in My Day "Perfect Boxes."

6. Broom and rake hooks—hardware stores will have these, too.

7. One to four plastic trash cans, for uses *other* than trash

8. Two to six empty coffee cans.

9. Black marking pen.

10. Three trash bags marked "Put Away," "Throw Away," and "Give Away."

How to Begin

1. Set a date. Example: Saturday, 9 A.M. Call a family meeting and ask the family to help "poor mom" clean the garage.

2. Make a list of all jobs.

3. Delegate responsibilities to each member of the family. Responsibilities could be written on pieces of paper and put into a basket. Have each family member, friend, neighbor, cat, dog, or whomever you can get to help, draw three jobs from the basket.

An Example

1. Jenny: Sort the nails and screws into different jars or into the metal organizational cabinet with the plastic drawers (that you purchased last week).

2. Brad: Separate hammers, screwdrivers, wrenches, and small tools into piles, then put them into the empty coffee cans that you have prelabeled with the black marking pen.

3. Husband Bob: Sort your possessions—papers, pipes, bolts, etc.—and put them into jars and cardboard boxes. Label with the black marking pen.

4. Craig: Neatly roll up the hoses, extension cords, wires, ropes, and any other roll-up type of materials.

Put all gardening tools with long handles (such as rake, shovel, edger, broom, etc.) down into one of the trash cans, or hang these tools on a wall in the garage with the special hooks purchased especially for them.

5. Dori: Empty the large bag of dried dog food into another of the plastic trash cans with a tight lid. It will keep fresh and prevent little animals such as mice from enjoying the food.

6. Mark (your ten-year-old neighbor boy): Collect all the clean rags, old towels, sheets, etc., and put those into a trash can with a lid or into a cardboard box marked accordingly.

7. Mom: Label the cardboard boxes and arrange them on shelves (hopefully you have some) in the garage according to priority. For example: You don't need the Christmas ornament boxes on the lower shelf because you will only get them down once a year, so they should be put on a top shelf.

More Suggestions

Bicycles can be hung on rafters with the large hooks you purchased at the hardware store. Most regular cars will easily drive under them. These are for bicycles not used every day. Maybe Dad or an older son could make a bike rack for the other bikes used most often.

The partially used bags of cement, fertilizer, and other dry materials can also be stored in the plastic trash cans with lids. This will prevent the materials from getting wet.

Gardening pots, bricks, flats, etc., can be neatly stored on a shelf in the garage or outside the garage in a convenient spot—or build a few shelves outside just for those things. Winter weather won't hurt them, and you have little need for them during those months anyway.

We must not forget the trash bags marked "Put Away," "Throw Away," and "Give Away." Be sure to fill them. You'll be finding newspapers, magazines, and empty or dried-up cans of paint. Put those types of things in the Throw Away trash bag—and throw them away!

You will also find many items which are perfectly good but which you never or seldom use. Put these into the Give Away bag and divide them up among neighbors, youth groups, needy families, thrift shops, churches, etc., or else have a garage sale and make a little extra money.

Whenever we have a garage sale we let the children keep whatever money comes from their items, such as outgrown games and toys, ice skates, clothing, etc. This encourages them to clean out and get rid of little-used items. Be careful, however, because children can get overexcited and sell their bed, desk, cat, or even baby brother!

The Put Away trash bag will have items you'll need to store in cardboard boxes, such as athletic equipment (mitts, baseballs, baseball caps, Frisbees, cleats, etc.). Another box will house the ice skates, mittens, snow caps, ski sweaters, thermal underwear, and wool socks. Be sure to throw in a few mothballs and label the boxes as to what's inside.

Another good way to label the boxes is to mark the items on 3" x 5" white cards and tape or staple the cards on the front of the boxes.

When storing clothing, you may want to put the clothes in a small trash bag with a few whole cloves, then into the cardboard storage box. This prevents silverfish and other little critters from having a picnic.

Spray-paint cans and smaller paint cans can be put into a storage box and labeled, too.

Are you beginning to feel all boxed up? Great! That

will free you from the guilt feelings of garage disorganization, and you'll now know where everything is.

Sweep and hose out any leftovers. Put hamburgers on the barbecue, then kick back and enjoy your family, being thankful that you worked well together!

Part

3

More Hours...
and Resource Savers

22

Dollar Mistakes to Avoid

*You may say to yourself, "My power
and the strength of my hands
have produced this wealth for me."
But remember the LORD your God,
for it is he who gives you
the ability to produce wealth.*

Deuteronomy 8:17,18, NIV

ࢠ —— ࢠ

Are you someone who just can't pass up a good deal: that special high-tech equipment, another camera gadget, one more power tool, another set of golf clubs, or an all-weather coat you can't do without?

We've all had that extra impulse that makes us go faster into debt, slowly sinking our money ship. These all seem like small expenditures, but do we really need them?

In *The 15-Minute Money Manager*,[1] we go to great lengths to describe how an individual or a family can manage money properly. In that book we talk about "Four Cornerstones for Money Management." They are:

- *Recognize that God owns everything.* He owns our home, our car, our marriage, our children, our 'job, our business, and our talents. We may possess them, but we don't own them. Possession is not ownership. In Haggai 2:8 (NIV) God states, "The silver is mine and the gold is mine," and Psalm 24:1 (NASB) properly states, "The earth is the LORD's, and all it contains, the world, and those who dwell in it."

- *The goal of financial responsibility is financial free-dom.* In order to be financially free you must meet these qualifications: Your income exceeds your expenses; you are able to pay your debts as they fall due; you have no unpaid bills; and, above all, you are content at your present income level.

- *Establish a spiritual purpose for your life.* If your spiritual purpose is to serve God (Matthew 6:33), all of your resources minister toward that end. The more money we give to God's work, the more our hearts will be fixed on Him. The opposite is also true: Don't give money to God's work, and your heart will not be fixed on Him.

- *Give money to the Lord on a regular basis.* God doesn't care how much we give as deeply as He cares *why* we give. When we lovingly and obediently fulfill our role as givers, no matter what the amount, God will use what we give to minister to others and we will receive a blessing in return. The Scripture clearly shows us many directions for our giving:

   —To God through our tithes, gifts, and offer-ings (Proverbs 3:9,10; 1 Corinthians 16:2)

   —To the poor (Proverbs 19:17)

   —To other believers in need (Romans 12:13; Galatians 6:9,10)

   —To those who minister to us (Galatians 6:6; 1 Timothy 5:17,18)

—To widows (1 Timothy 5:3-16)

—To family members (1 Timothy 5:8)

With the above direction set for our money management, let's look at some common financial mistakes that we make, which in the long run cost us a lot of money:

1. *Attempting to make it rich too fast.* There is no quick way to get rich. If it's too good to be true, it's probably not true. Stay away from quick ways to make a dollar. So many people have been taken in by smooth-talking salesmen. Build up sales resistance by saying "no."

2. *Believing the credit-card delusion.* Credit on the credit cards does not make you have a higher standard of living—it will be the ruin of your finances. With rare exceptions, don't charge any more than you can pay off when the bill comes due.

3. *Not taking advantage of your benefit plans at work.* Most companies offer employee 401(k) or 403(b) saving plans, which permit you to avoid paying current taxes while saving money for retirement. Talk to your personnel office at work to see if your company has such a plan. If not, consider opening one yourself if you are self-employed, or open your own IRA plan.

4. *Overpaying your house payment (mortgage).* If you didn't refinance your home mortgage recently when interest rates were at an all-time low, you are probably overpaying your monthly mortgage. You can reduce your house payment significantly by refinancing. Shop around to see what interest rates are available. Start out with your present lender and go from there.

5. *Overinsuring your insurance (auto, home, life, and health).* Review with each of your carriers to see if you can reduce your premiums. In some cases you may be buying more coverage than you need. It also provides you an

opportunity to re-evaluate where you need more coverage than you presently have.

6. *Investing for your children's college education the wrong way.* With any investment toward college, make sure the account is using your child's own Social Security number and not yours. If not, you will be paying taxes on all interest and dividends earned each year. This will be costing you more than it has to. You can save most of this interest tax by having the money or investments in a "custodian" account that carries your child's Social Security number. This could be called "Craig Merrihew as custodian for Christine Merrihew, a minor," under the Uniform Gift to Minors Act. Under present tax laws, the first 600 dollars of interest and dividends earned each year in such an account is tax-free. Check with your local bank or a stock brokerage house in your area.

7. *Falling for a "hot tip."* Avoid these with a passion. Don't invest your hard-earned money in anything that you don't understand. *Never* be swayed by a phone solicitor. Only deal with reputable parties, and make sure you understand the offering. Request a copy of the prospectus. Read thoroughly and ask all your questions first before you give any money.

And now for some money-management practices to follow:

1. *Maintain excellent credit.* Protect this status as if it were gold. If your credit report contains improper information, take care of that immediately. If not, it will delay or prevent you from getting a loan or delay the refinancing of your home mortgage.

TRW, the largest of the three major credit bureaus, will send you a free copy of your credit report. Write to: TRW Consumer Assistance, P.O. Box 2350, Chatsworth, CA

91313-2350; or call 1-800-392-1122. Include verification of your full name and present address (a copy of your driver's license or utility bill is fine), all previous addresses for the past five years (no verification required), your Social Security number, date of birth, and spouse's first name.

Equifax charges $8 in most states for a copy of your report. Write to: Equifax Information Service Center, P.O. Box 740241, Atlanta, GA 30374; or call 1-800-685-1111. Include your full name, current and previous addresses, Social Security number, date of birth, and telephone number.

Trans Union also charges $8 (free if you've been denied credit), or $16 if you request a report for your spouse as well as yourself. Write to: Trans Union Corporation, P.O. Box 7000, North Olmstead, OH 44070; or call 216-779-2378. Include your full name, current and previous addresses (for the past two years), Social Security number, date of birth, current place of employment, and telephone number. Your credit report from all three of these companies will include instructions on how to correct any errors.[2]

2. *Keep your money invested in areas that provide good returns.* If most of your money is in no- or low-interest checking or money market accounts that pay anywhere from 1 to 2.5 percent interest, think about shifting that money into five-year CD's, or purchasing U.S. Treasury EE bonds. For a small risk, consider short-term bond funds or short-term U.S. Treasury notes. Call a good brokerage firm in your area for added information. Many larger banks are now offering these same services. Talk to your present banker.

3. *Keep good financial records.* They don't have to be fancy, but they need to be saved in a fashion where you

can be sure to deduct the expenses on your tax return. Keep track of home improvements so you will have proof of these expenses when you get ready to sell that home. Listing home improvement costs will lower your profits and you will pay less tax on your capital gain. All it takes is a simple log recording the date of each improvement, what it was, how much it cost you, with a running total in the last column—very easy, and it takes just a few minutes. Be sure to keep your receipts for these improvements.

4. *If married, make sure your mate is part of the money-management process.* How often have I had a lady friend lose a husband to disability or death and know very little about the family's finances. Make sure that each of you are involved in these decisions and that you know what's happening.

5. *Be willing to take a few risks.* This is different than the "too-good-to-be-true" story. A well-balanced portfolio will have a diversified approach to stocks, bonds, CDs, real estate, and money-market accounts. You might want to consider keeping some of your savings in investments with growth potential. You can choose stocks or mutual funds for some of your personal savings. Again, check with your bank or stockbroker.

6. *Be sure to leave a trust or a will.* Contact a local attorney who specializes in these and set up a date and time for your meeting. This is so very important in order to leave your estate to those you want to benefit from your lifetime of work. Shop around for prices, however—it's not as expensive as you might think (varies upon the complexity of your estate).

23

Bulk Buying—Money and Time Savings

Turn to Me and be saved,
all the ends of the earth;
for I am God, and there is no other.

Isaiah 45:22, NASB

❧ —— ❧

My Bob teases me when we go out to one of the large discount stores and it costs 150 dollars to get out the door. He jokes that it is "free getting in, but costs our family inheritance to get out." It's true that you pay more up front, but it saves you so much in money and time later on.

Rushing off to the store every time you need an item wastes time, energy, and money. You spend time driving and waiting in line and end up spending more money than you intended.

By purchasing nonperishable items in bulk (and when they are on sale), you will spend less unscheduled time at the store, seldom run out of necessities, and save money by buying in bulk. Buying by the case or in large quantities usually costs less than buying single items.

Take stress out of your life by keeping these items on hand:

- Paper products such as greeting cards, gift-wrapping paper, ribbon, and boxes and strapping tape for mailing

- Extra school supplies
- Tape and glue
- Pet food
- Envelopes (legal and letter size)
- Paper plates, plastic glasses, and plastic forks, spoons, and knives
- Special-occasion and party supplies such as birthday candles
- Small gifts for friends, neighbors, and holiday drop-ins
- Postage stamps
- Shampoo and soap
- Toothpaste, toothbrushes, and mouthwash
- Laundry supplies
- Cleaning supplies
- Canned and bottled foods, condiments, and soft drinks
- Basic dry foods
- Blank videotapes
- Film and camera batteries
- Various sizes of light bulbs
- Candles
- Various sizes of paper and plastic bags (recycle the ones you get at the market)

24

Space-Saver Ideas

*Any kingdom divided against itself
will be ruined, and a house
divided against itself will fall.*

Luke 11:17, NIV

❧ —— ❧

One of the first comments that women make to me about home management is, "But I don't have space! We live in a small home (or apartment, or mobile home)." Most of us do live in a smaller residence than we would like. That's when you really have to work smart.

This chapter will help you stretch that small space. It will amaze you what a little preplanning can do for you.

Living Areas

- Install a towel rack on the inside of the linen-closet door to hang tablecloths.

- Remodel an antique armoire to house your entertainment center (TV, CD player, VCR components). An armoire also works great for extra closet space in a bedroom.

- Use my "Perfect Boxes" covered with wallpaper matching your room colors. These will accommodate a lot of storage items. Stack three of these boxes on top of each other, place a circular plywood round on top, cover with a colorful fabric from tabletop to floor, and you have a very attractive end or corner table. (See the "Total Mess to Total Rest" chapter.)

- Hang your stereo speakers on a wall to free up space on the floor or on a shelf.

- Use the tops of cabinets, hutches, and refrigerator to store floral arrangements or other attractive items (to make excellent designer areas).

- Build a window seat under deep-set windows, and use the space underneath for storage.

- Use under the stairs for added storage. Remember to install shelves—you'll get a lot of boxes off the floor.

- Put tall, slim bookcases in a room to create storage shelves.

Bedrooms

- Move some of the children's sports equipment out of their bedrooms into the garage, attic, or basement. Store these items in large, plastic trash bins or on wall hooks.

- Use egg-carton bottoms or ice-cube trays to organize small items in drawers.

- The early Shaker settlers used wooden dowels around their rooms to hang clothing. We have these and they work great.

- Seldom-used luggage is ideal for storing out-of-season clothing.

- We have a motto: "A new item of clothes purchased, an old item given away to someone in need."

- Convert an antique armoire into a cabinet to store sweaters, bulky shirts, or whatever else will fit.

- Use the space under beds to store boxes of overflow items. My "Perfect Boxes" are a great fit for this space.

- Build a plate shelf or book rack 9″ to 12″ wide up high on the walls around your room. A lot of decorative items can be stored here.

- Stack "Perfect Boxes" beside the bed to double as nightstands. Cover these with a plywood round and nice fabric to match your bedroom colors.

- Select a headboard for your bed that has storage space.

- Go through your bedroom at least once a quarter and reorganize this area of your home. Toss out items not being used.

Clothes Closets

- Redo your single-clothes-rod closet to accommodate the new closet organizers. You can really improve closet efficiency.

- Keep clothes that need mending in a designated place (such as the laundry area). Keep on top of the mending. Don't let it pile up on you.

- Store off-season clothes in another closet or in a trunk not in the main closet. If your children are grown and no longer home, you could use their closets for this. If you store clothes in your attic or basement, be sure to guard against mildew.

- Put hooks on the wall inside the closet to hang nightgowns, robes, and shoulder bags.

- Hang a battery-operated rotating tie rack from your husband's top rod. This can store a lot of ties, and the ties can be exhibited by pressing a button.

- Install a mug rack on the closet wall for small hats, purses, and scarves.

- When redoing your closet into a space-saver unit, have some vertical shoe storage racks built in (make sure they are wide enough to accommodate two pairs of shoes side by side).

- Take heavy boots out of the closet area and set them close to the door for seasonal use.

- Hang a mesh laundry bag with a drawstring for dirty hose and lingerie. Toss the full bag into the washer on the "delicate" cycle.

Children's Closet

- Use hangers and storage bins to color-coordinate your children's belongings. Get towels in each child's color. This saves a lot of identification time. They can easily see what is theirs.

- Keep small, everyday clothing items in their colorful plastic bins on reachable shelves.

- Store a small step stool in the closet to help children reach high shelves.

- Install a commercially built closet organizer that has one rod to store long hanging clothes, separated by shelving for storage. On the other side, have two rods for shorter clothing and out-of-season clothing. Put often-worn clothing on the lower rod.

- Get color-coordinated child-size hangers. The children can handle them easier and are more likely to hang up their clothes.

- Use a lot of hooks inside the closets so the children can hang robes, nightclothes, and coats.

- Build a shelf that runs across the back or side of the closet to keep shoes organized.

- Compliment the children when they keep their clothing picked up.

- Let your children help you redecorate their rooms. They will take more pride in their areas if they have had a part in the selection of colors, wallpapers, and fabrics.

Storage Space

- Organize and store items in places convenient for their use. Store like things together. Arrange frequently used objects on waist-to-eye-level shelves, in drawers, or on hooks. Try not to bend or reach more than necessary. Before you buy something new, make sure you know where it will be stored.

- Identify nontraditional storage areas in your home: an old trunk, a sink cavity, a high plate rail around a room, as well as under beds, under staircases, and in attics, basements, or garages. Consider attaching racks to the back of closet and pantry doors.

- Study your storage situation and ask yourself these basic questions:

  —Has the item been worn or used in the last year?

  —Does the item have personal or monetary value?

—Will the item be worn or used again in the near future?

If your answer is "no" to anyone of the questions don't store the item in prime space. One of our mottos is: "Less is best."

• Before you add more *stuff* to your limited space, ask yourself a few basic questions:

—Do I really need this stuff?

—How often will I use it?

—How much space will be required to store it?

—Does it need to be cared for? How much care is needed?

If you don't need it or can't store it, don't buy it. When it comes to gift time in our family, we tell the children not to give us anything that needs storage, dusting, or attention (in other words, we only want consumable items— not storage items). We have enough *stuff*.

25

Earth-Saver Ideas

*And God saw all that He had made,
and behold, it was very good.
And there was evening and
there was morning, the sixth day.*

Genesis 1:31, NASB

&. ——— &.

We live in a period of time where we are very conscious about our environment and the depletion of some of our most valuable resources. Make conservation a family project. The children will think that it's neat, because that's what they are talking about in school.

All of these ideas can't be implemented at one time, but choose a new one each week and keep practicing the old ones. Children really like being involved in these projects.

Here are a few ideas that will make our world safer from "progress pollution":

- *Say "no."* Don't purchase disposable products that aren't degradable.

- *Separate your trash.* Cooperate with your local waste-management programs.

- *Fix leaky faucets and toilets.* You don't think a little drop adds up to very much but it does. In fact, a leaky faucet can waste 3000 gallons of water a year, and a leaky toilet can use an extra 20,000 gallons a year—enough to fill a good-size swimming pool.

- *Use paper bags instead of plastic.* Paper is easier to recycle.

- *Flush the solid waste before tossing disposable diapers.*

- *Recycle bottles and cans.* Not only does recycling clean up the waste, but it can also be a great way to earn some extra money.

- *Carpool to work.* Over 33 percent of all private vehicle mileage is due to work travel. Carpooling can save gas and cut down on pollution, plus greatly decrease automobile expenses.

- *Drive less.* Walk, cycle, or use mass transit more often.

- *Turn the lights out.* Get the whole family used to turning off the light switch when leaving a room.

- *Limit use of your garbage disposal.* It uses a lot of water, plus the garbage has to be removed at the sewage plant. Start a compost pile for all your waste.

- *Scrutinize packaging.* If sending a package, don't use a lot of excess paper or Styrofoam. Encourage manufacturers not to package their products with excess packing.

- *Turn your water heater to the lowest setting* and turn it off when you go on long trips.

- *Dress appropriately.* Reduce your heating and air-conditioning needs by wearing the right clothing. It's healthier to keep your house on the cool side. Lap blankets are great when relaxing for the evening.

- *Try composting.* It's amazing how many pounds of compost a family can generate in a year. Your plants will love the nutrients you add to the soil. The compost also reduces the amount of water needed per plant.

- *Set your sprinklers properly.* Make sure the water hits the plants and not the sidewalks, streets, or driveways.

- *Pick up litter.* Not only does it make the area look clean, but removing litter can also prevent someone from tripping or having an accident.

- *Take a shower—not a bath.* Surprisingly, a shower uses only half the amount of water that a bath does.

- *Use canvas bags to do your grocery shopping.* They're much better than paper or plastic, plus they're reusable and don't create any waste.

- *Shop big.* Buy products in larger sizes rather than in a lot of smaller cartons. There will be less waste.

- *Pull out weeds by hand.* This saves on sprays with toxic waste that gets into the water supply.

- *Don't hose down the sidewalks or driveways.* Use a blower or broom to clean these areas. For every minute your hose is on, you are using three-fifths of a gallon of water.

- *Don't overcool.* A lot of people keep their refrigerators too cold, thus using unnecessary energy. Refrigerators should be kept at 40° F. and the freezer at 5° F. (Use ice cream to test your freezer compartment. If it's too soft, set the freezer slightly colder; if too hard, set the control slightly warmer).

- *Take care with your wash.* Use biodegradable products. Phosphates contribute to the growth of algae.

- *Don't preheat the oven.* If your recipe will take more than one hour to cook, you can start in a cold oven. You can also turn your oven off before your meal is cooked. The oven will retain the heat to finish the cooking. However, when cooking cakes and pastries you should preheat.

- *Look for energy-efficient appliances.* As your old appliances wear out, look for those that have an energy-efficient rating.

- *Reuse paper.* You can always use the back of papers for notes. Take these sheets that have writing on one side and cut them into fourths. Staple the sheets together, and you have a zero-cost notepad.

- *Flush little—not big.* For most standard toilets, you flush six gallons of water down the drain. Fill an old plastic bottle with water and put it or a brick in the tank to use less water.

- *Wash your car from a bucket.* Fill a gallon bucket of warm water with a few drops of auto wash detergent. Use a soft terrycloth rag to wash the car, and use a large (beach) towel to dry the car. Start at the top and work down. This technique can save from 100 to 150 gallons of water.

- *Plant a tree.* Our countryside and cities need more trees. Plant one for any occasion. Trees take in carbon dioxide and produce oxygen.

- *Recycle newspaper.* Many communities have area newspaper recycling dumps. It only takes a minute to drop newspapers off, but it will save cutting down excess trees.

- *Stop unwanted junk mail.* Thousands of tons of paper are used to mail out junk mail. If you want to stop the waste, write: Mail Preference Service, District Marketing Assoc., 6 East 43rd St., New York, NY 10017.

- *Recycle old items you aren't using.* When you do your "Total Mess to Total Rest" program, take those Give Away items that are not being used and recycle them by giving them to charity or by selling them at a garage sale.

- *Recharge those batteries.* With more and more toys and equipment using batteries as a power source, buy rechargeable ones rather than those that are disposable.

- *Clean your dryer screens.* A clogged screen makes the dryer work harder, using as much as 20 percent more energy to dry one load of clothes.

- *Conserve water while brushing your teeth.* Even though it's one of Amercica's biggest habits, turn off the faucet when you are brushing your teeth.

- *Let solar heat work for your.* During the winter open your curtains, draperies, and blinds. This way the sun can help heat your home.

- *Keep curtains closed.* You can have a cooler home during the summertime if you close your blinds, drapes, and curtains during the day or while gone from your home for a long period of time.

- *Use attic fans to help reduce your cooling costs.* Our attics are pockets for catching extreme heat during those long, hot days of summer. Install one or more thermostat-controlled attic fans.

- *Weatherstrip your windows and doors.* For a few dollars you can purchase weatherstripping from your local hardware store. This will drastically cut down your energy bills each month.

- *Close that unused damper in the fireplace.* Fires are beautiful and give some low-cost heating, but if the damper is left open when you aren't using the fireplace, you have an unseen shaft that lets valuable energy escape from your home.

- *Install ceiling fans.* If you haven't been introduced to the efficiency of a ceiling fan, go out and talk to the fan representative at one of the many stores which carry these. Ceiling fans are excellent for summer and winter usage, and turn on with just a flip of a switch.

26

Free Water-Saving Ideas

God called the dry ground, "land,"
and the gathered waters he called "seas."
And God saw that it was good.

Genesis 1:10, NIV

❧ —— ❧

Little did we ever think that California would have a water crisis, but we recently went through a severe water shortage. Some areas were restricted on when and how much water they could use on a daily basis. Many communities imposed large fines if you used more water than was allocated to you.

Not only should we be aware of misusing water, but as informed consumers we need to be sensitive to the fact that water costs us money.

Let's not only conserve water because it is a valuable resource, but let's reduce our consumption and save money.

These simple water-saving steps (adapted from a 1993 Metropolitian Water District of Southern California pamphlet) can cut hundreds of gallons out of your weekly usage. Whether you want to cut back 15, 25 or even 50 percent, the more steps you take, the more you'll save. It's easier than you think to save water.

In the Bathroom

- While waiting for hot water to come down the pipes, catch the cool water in a bucket or watering can. You can use it later to water plants, run your garbage disposal, or pour into the toilet bowl to flush it (saves 50 gallons a week per person).

- Replace your regular showerheads with low-flow showerheads (saves 230 gallons a week).

- Keep your showers down to five minutes or less (saves 75 gallons a week per person).

- Turn the water off while lathering in the shower. Then turn the water back on to quickly rinse (saves 75 gallons a week per person).

- Take shallow baths—no more than three inches of water (saves 100 gallons a week per person).

- Replace your regular toilets with new ultra-low-flush models (saves 350 gallons a week).

- Put a water displacement device inside the tank of every toilet. You can make one with a plastic bottle of water weighted down with pebbles (saves 50 gallons a week for each toilet).

- Check your toilets for leaks. Drop a dye tablet or a teaspoon of food coloring in the tank. If the color appears in the bowl after 15 minutes, replace the "flapper" valve (saves 100 gallons a week for each toilet repaired).

- Flush the toilet only when necessary. And never use the toilet as an ash tray or wastebasket (saves 150 gallons a week).

- Don't let the water run while brushing your teeth or shaving (saves 35 gallons a week per person).

In the Kitchen

- Hand wash dishes just once a day using the least amount of detergent possible. This will cut down on rinsing. Use a sprayer or short blasts of water to rinse (saves 100 gallons a week).

- If you have a dishwasher, run it only when you have a full load (saves 30 gallons a week).

- Scrape food scraps off dishes into the garbage can or rinse them off with very short blasts of hot water (saves 60 gallons a week).

- Run your garbage disposal only on alternate days (saves 25 gallons a week).

- Rinse vegetables and fruits in a sink or pan filled with water instead of under running water (saves 30 gallons a week).

Around the House

- Repair all leaky faucets, fixtures, and pipes both inside and outside your home (saves 150 gallons a week for each leak).

- When doing the laundry, never wash less than a full load (saves 100 gallons a week).

- Collect washing machine rinse water in utility sink. You can use it later to water indoor plants, run your garbage disposal, or pour into the toilet bowl to flush it (saves 50 gallons a week).

Outdoors

- Water your lawn and landscaping no more than once a week. Only water early in the morning or after the sun sets, when there's less evaporation (saves 250 gallons a week).

- Deactivate automatic sprinklers and operate them manually. Adjust your sprinklers so they don't spray on sidewalks, driveway, or street (saves 250 gallons a week).

- Set lawn mower blades one notch higher since longer grass reduces evaporation. Use chunks of bark, peat moss, or gravel to cover bare ground in gardens and around trees (saves 200 gallons a week).

- Never hose off your driveway, patio, or sidewalk— use a broom instead (saves 100 gallons or more a week).

- Don't allow your children to play with the hose (saves 10 gallons a minute).

- If you have a pool, use a cover to cut down evaporation. This will also keep your pool cleaner and reduce the need to add chemicals (saves 250 gallons a week).

- Take your car to a car wash that recycles its wash water. If home car-washing is permitted in your area, use a bucket of water and a sponge. Rinse the car quickly at the end. Never allow the hose to run continuously (saves 150 gallons a week).

27

Investing Made Easy

*Why then didn't you put my money
on deposit, so that when I came back,
I could have collected it with interest?*

Luke 19:23, NIV

❧ —— ❧

While writing *The 15-Minute Money Manager* (published by Harvest House), Bob and I realized that people are in a hurry and often don't take time to manage many phases of their lives properly. One of the most surprising areas was that of finance.

We have often heard of very successful people—professional athletes, actors, writers, speakers, doctors, and other professionals—who have high incomes but then go broke or lose large sums of money because they didn't pay attention to small details. Of all the activities that you cram into your daily schedule, managing your money is the one you can least afford to overlook.

Here are several quick, worry-free techniques that will help you manage your money with less stress.

1. *Company Saving Plans.* This is one of the sweetest ways to see your money grow. Where else can you go where your employer matches your own contributions? Under this type of plan you sign an authorization card

requesting that your employer invest a certain percentage of your salary through automatic payroll deductions. The big plus is that your employer usually matches part or all of your contributions. Most of these types of plans have a 401(k) feature which means some of your contribution is tax-deferred and reduces your taxable income.

You will pay no tax on your boss's matching contribution until you withdraw it at the time of retirement or when you leave the company. If you resign from the company before you are fully vested (usually two to six years), you are not eligible to take out your employers matching contribution.

2. *Dollar Cost Averaging.* This is a great technique for the person who doesn't want to spend a great amount of time tracking individual stocks. Choose a stock or a mutual fund that meets your financial goals criteria for the next five to ten years.

We waste a lot of time trying to choose just the right time to purchase stock. Is the cost high? When will it be low? With the dollar-cost-averaging technique you invest a fixed amount (say 75 dollars) every month regardless of whether the price of shares is going down or going up. Over a long period of time—five to ten years—you will find the cost per share will even out to the medium price of the stock.

This type of purchase avoids two common errors: investing all your money when prices are up and selling out at a loss when prices are low.

To simplify this technique, you can authorize payroll deductions or a checking-account transfer between your company or bank and a certain mutual fund or individual stock of your choice.

3. *Prepay Your Mortgage.* "You mean to say that an extra 25 dollars a month on my house payment will save

me $18,221 on a $100,000.00 30-year loan at seven percent interest?" Yes, it does, and if you are able to contribute more than that you will get a more remarkable savings of interest. This discipline really works. Sit down with your mortgage holder and review the figures to see what plan would be best for your financial position. Most mortgages no longer carry prepayment penalties. Check with your mortgage agreement or call your lender to find out if any restrictions apply.

When I write my check each month for our house payment, I include an extra amount and I put a note with my check stating that I want the extra money to go to reduce my principal.

4. *Dividend Reinvestment Plans.* This is one of the great techniques of owning stock (available in over 1000 companies) without paying commission to a broker. These companies let you invest your quarterly dividends in purchasing additional shares, without charging you any fees. Many of these companies will also give you a five-to-ten dollar discount on the price of the stock.

On top of the quarterly reinvestment of dividends, you have the opportunity to contribute X number of dollars for added purchases. Each company will have its own monthly or yearly limitation amounts.

To participate in this type of program, you need to initially own one to one hundred shares, depending on the company.

Send two dollars to Public Relations Department, Standard and Poor's Corp., 25 Broadway, New York, NY 10004, and they will send you a list of companies which offer this type of plan.

5. *Asset-Management Accounts.* This is a great way to track all of your investment income and securities transactions for a year. The bank or brokerage firm which offers this service sends very detailed listings of all these

transactions. At the end of the year you have a comprehensive summary for tax purposes. Many of these services will even list your deductible expenses and capital gains and losses.

This type of account will combine a brokerage margin account with a money-market account, a checking account, and a credit card. Most of these accounts offer unlimited free checking, plus a debit or credit card to make purchases or withdraw cash at banks and ATMs worldwide. Some plans let you deposit your paycheck and have your fixed monthly bills paid automatically.

Dividends, interest, deposits, and proceeds from the sale of your stocks are automatically invested in a taxable or tax-free money fund.

6. *Automatic Payroll Deduction Plans*. Very little effort is involved in this type of plan. If your employer doesn't offer this type of savings program, check with your bank or credit union to see if they do. You simply fill out an authorization form, and your bank will deduct a certain amount from your checking account on the day you so designate and transfer it to an IRA, money-market fund, savings account, or EE savings bonds.

7. *A Company Profit-Sharing Plan*. This type of investing varies with the kind of company you work for. Company plans vary, but many do offer an easy way to plan for retirement. Check with your personnel office for details.

Some companies distribute a certain part of profits as a yearly bonus, but many will hold the profits in trust as a retirement plan for you. The tax advantage to this type of program is that you pay no taxes until you withdraw the shares from your account. Many of these profit-sharing plans allow voluntary contributions under a 401(k) option.

8. *Employee Stock Purchase Plans.* If you work for a company that offers this type of program, you are eligible to purchase shares of your company's stock on a regular basis. There usually aren't any administrative or commission charges for such transactions. One advantage to this type of investment is that you're not taxed on any gain or loss until you sell the stock. Most plans won't permit you to borrow against your account or take out cash until you retire or terminate your employment.

9. *Deferred-Pay 401(k) Plans.* If your company offers this type of plan, you want to jump on the bandwagon as quickly as possible. This type of program helps you reduce your taxable income by making a portion non-reportable on your W-2 form. Your earnings are compounded and tax-deferred, too. You may contribute up to $9,235 a year (indexed for inflation). Many companies will match all or part of your contributions.

The downside is that you may not withdraw funds until you reach age 59, or you'll get hit by a 10 percent penalty, unless the funds are rolled over into an IRA account within 60 days.

The only way to avoid a 20 percent withholding fee by the IRS when you withdraw funds from this account is by:

- Depositing the full amount into an IRA within 60 days, or
- Telling your employer to transfer your money directly into an IRA.

These techniques will help you reduce the stress of having to invest large amounts of time in managing your finances. May I also recommend that you read *The 15-Minute Money Manager*, written by my husband Bob and me (Eugene, OR: Harvest House Publishers, 1993).

28

Tips on Brightening Your Home for Sale

*For we walk by faith,
not by sight.*

2 Corinthians 5:7, NASB

ᴥ —— ᴥ

As we look around our neighborhood, there are always a few "For Sale" signs in our neighbors' yards. For various reasons, the American public is on the move. Most people will relocate every five years. Selling a home quickly for the right price meets with a lot of competition with others in your neighborhood. Why would anyone want to buy your home over someone else's?

Let your home smile a welcome to buyers. With a little effort on your part, your home can be sold more quickly and at a better price.

These 19 tips have proved invaluable to owners and are worth your special attention.

Preparation for Showing

- *First impressions are lasting.* The front door greets the prospect. Make sure it is fresh, clean, and scrubbed-looking. Keep lawn trimmed and edged, and the yard free of refuse. Be sure snow and ice are removed from walks and steps.

- *Decorate for a quick sale.* Faded walls and worn wood-work reduce appeal. Why try to tell the prospect how your home could look, when you can show him by redecorating? A quicker sale at a higher price will result. An investment in new kitchen wallpaper will pay dividends.

- *Let the sun shine in.* Open draperies and curtains and let the prospect see how cheerful your home can be. (Dark rooms are not appealing.)

- *Fix that faucet!* Dripping water discolors sinks and suggests faulty plumbing.

- *Repairs can make a big difference.* Loose knobs, sticking doors and windows, warped cabinet drawers, and other minor flaws detract from a home's value. Have them fixed.

- *Remove clutter from top to bottom.* Display the full value of your attic, basement, and other utility space by removing all unnecessary articles. Brighten a dark, dull basement by painting the walls.

- *Put safety first.* Keep stairways clear. Avoid a cluttered appearance and possible injuries.

- *Make closets look bigger.* Neat, well-ordered closets show that the space is ample.

- *Bathrooms help sell homes, so make these rooms sparkle.* Check and repair caulking in bathtubs and showers.

- *Arrange bedrooms neatly.* Remove excess furniture. Use attractive bedspreads and freshly laundered curtains.

- *Turn on all the lights.* Illumination is like a welcome sign. The potential buyer will feel a warm glow when your home is brightly lit for an evening inspection

- *Three's a crowd, so avoid having too many people present during inspections.* The potential buyer will feel like an intruder and will hurry through the house.

- *Keep the music mellow.* Turn off the blaring radio or television. Let the salesman and buyer talk free of loud disturbances.

- *Keep pets out of the way—preferably out of the house.*

- *Silence is golden.* Be courteous but don't force conversation with the potential buyer. He wants to inspect your house—not pay a social call.

- *Never apologize for the appearance of your home.* After all, it has been lived in. Let the trained salesman answer any objections. This is his job.

- *Stay in the background.* The salesman knows the buyer's requirements and can better emphasize the features of your home when you don't tag along. You will be called if needed.

- *Why put the cart before the horse?* Trying to dispose of furniture and furnishings to the potential buyer before he has purchased the house often loses a sale.

- *A word to the wise: Let your realtor discuss price, terms, possession, and other factors with the customer.* He/she is eminently qualified to bring negotiations to a favorable conclusion.

29

Ask First Before Buying That Home

Unless the LORD builds the house,
they labor in vain who build it;
unless the LORD guards the city,
the watchman keeps awake in vain.

Psalm 127:1, NASB

❧ —— ❧

Huse purchasing is a very emotional experience. We have visualized what that dream home is going to look like: what color it will be, what trees will be in the front yard, and the layout of the landscaping. Before we buy a home, we will probably have considered if we want automatic sprinklers, an attic with useable space, and a finished basement.

As we visit various homes, we may find the dream home, but it may not be correct for us. When deciding upon that home, there is more to consider than dream expectations.

When purchasing a home, you can do a lot to narrow down the choices by using this checklist. Ask yourself the following questions *before* you put down a deposit.

General Impressions

- What do you like best about the home?

- What do you like least about the house? Can these disadvantages be corrected?

245

- Will this home be a low-, medium-, or high-maintenance home? Will your budget allow for proper maintenance?

Space and Circulation

- Is there enough bedroom/closet/bathroom space? It's often easier and cheaper to buy a larger home than to add rooms later.

- How is the traffic flow through the house?

- Is there an easy route to get groceries from the car to the kitchen?

- Can muddy or sandy feet go directly to a service porch or utility room before going to the living area?

- How well are sounds controlled in the house? Can you hear toilets flush, the dishwasher go through its cycle, or sounds of an entertainment center throughout the home?

Neighborhood and Locale

- Visit the neighborhood during different times of the day.

- Is the home close to schools, churches, and shopping, with easy access to freeways or toll roads?

- How noisy is it during peak traffic times?

- Are there evidences of children the ages of your own in the neighborhood?

- Check out the quality of education offered in the neighborhood school.

- What do the homes next door to you and those across the street look like?

- Knock on a neighbor's door and ask how he or she likes the neighborhood.

- See where the sun exposure will be during different seasons of the year. This is very important if you live in areas of climatic extremes, or if you are a gardener and want proper sun exposure during the growing season.

Condition

- How old is the roof? Are you in a fire hazard area? If so, do you have a fire-retardant roof?

- In what condition is the furnace? Ask to see utility bills from the last 12 months.

- If the area gets extremely hot, does the house have central air-conditioning? If not, what would be the cost to have it installed?

- Is the garage adequate for your needs? Is there a garage-door opener? Is there room to hold cars, lawn equipment, ladders, children's bicycles, and snow equipment (if needed for your area)?

- Are there any problems with mildew or wetness in the basement, termites, material defects, bad septic system, water stains? Request that the seller furnish you with a passed inspection before the close of escrow.

Since a home is probably the largest purchase you will make in your lifetime, you want to take all the precautions that will give you a peace of mind. *Don't rush*—take your time. Make sure it's the right home with no hidden defects that will cause you difficulty in repairing or will cause you anxiety to live with.

In most geographic areas of our country, resales have slowed down. You want your home to be all that you anticipate it to be. Correcting the mistake of purchasing the wrong house is a slow and expensive proposition.

Part

4

More Hours...
for Family and
Friends

30

Develop Family Traditions

*For where your treasure is,
there your heart will be also.*

Matthew 6:21, NIV

❧ —— ❧

I often question ladies who attend my seminars about traditions they had in their families while growing up—traditions that set them apart as belonging to that unique family (a sign, a thumbs-up, a kiss on the nose, a pinch of the cheek). I found that most people had no such traditions. Some even asked, "What's a tradition?" or said "We had no traditions at all, even at Christmas time, birthdays, or anniversaries."

As you know by reading my many books, I am a strong believer in family traditions. I have found that it takes only small gestures to bring our family closer. They help you connect with your family and maintain those ties.

Many of these traditions have been used by our own family; others have been shared by ladies who have attended my seminars or who have read my books. There are probably more ideas than you can use. Select a few that interest you and try them on your family members. My Bob tells me that I am never too old to start a new tradition. So let's start now. . . .

A Butterfly Kiss

My Bob gives the grandchildren a "butterfly kiss" by fluttering his eyelids on the children's cheeks. They just love it. Another one (which I won't prescribe) is a "car-wash kiss." You can guess what that's like.

A Special Handshake

My Bob always greets a certain male friend and his two grown sons with a special greeting. They shake hands, slip down to a clasp of the finger tips, quickly move into a thumb grip, shift to a knock on the elbow, and finish with a big smile. Only men can do that—it's not very dainty for women.

Silent Communication

Invent a silent symbol of your family's camaraderie. For example, a thumbs-up, a wink, a tug on the earlobe.

Kid Fix

Request a "kid fix"—a hefty hug and a big kiss—whenever you feel the need. Let your youngsters know it makes you feel much better.

Once a Day

Tell your children you love them at least once every 24 hours—when you send them off to school, when they come home, when you pray with them at night, or any-time.

Go Ahead, Try It

Encourage your child to try new things—taste unusual foods, enter contests, write for information on subjects that interest him or her.

Double Desserts

Once a month, surprise your family by announcing double-dessert night.

Yogurt Run

During the summer or when the children don't have school the next day, go into their rooms just before they fall asleep and announce a "yogurt run." They will think you have flipped out, but they will always remember those special times when you got them out of bed and went to get some delightful yogurt.

You Are Special Today

We have a large red plate which has inscribed on it: "You Are Special Today." We are always honoring a member of the family or guest who comes to dinner. We've even taken this plate to restaurants, on a picnic, and to a beach party. We let that special person use the special plate. We also take a photograph of the person and place the picture in a special photo album that houses pictures of our recipients.

Another feature we have added to this tradition is to go around the table and have each person tell our honored guest why we think he or she is special. Then we let our special person tell us why he or she is special. It's amazing what has happened through this tradition.

Sharing a Secret

You can have a lot of fun by sharing a secret and then keeping up the suspense until Christmas or a birthday comes. It's also good training to teach the children how to keep a secret.

What's the Best Thing That Happened to You Today?

Quite often we ask this question toward the end of our meal, and the discussion that follows keeps the family together at the table for a longer time and keeps us talking. No TV is allowed during dinner.

Mom's Canned Questions

We have a jar of 150 questions that are great for the family to answer in a constructive way during any mealtime. Many times we even use this jar of questions when our adult friends come to visit.

Cooking Class

At least once a month set aside a special afternoon where the children are invited to the kitchen to prepare a meal or a portion of a meal. Desserts are always a winner. Bring out the aprons and chef's hat—if they dress like cooks, they will really get involved in the process.

Bravo!

Three cheers for success! Honor some child who does well in an activity, on a test or a term report, or by completing a chore. Make it a big deal—you might even cook the person's favorite meal.

Young Decorator

When sprucing up your children's rooms, allow them to pick the color theme, paint, sheets, curtains, or towels. If that's too risky, give them specific choices (several wallpaper designs, three or four paints, or choices of several bedspreads).

Study Hall

Select that special area at home—a table, a couch, a chair—for your children to review materials to be covered in a test tomorrow. Have them cozy up and get comfortable in their special "study hall."

What a Fine Family We Have

I'm one for framing family pictures all over the house—individuals and group pictures from last summer's vacation, a winter ski trip, or a Christmas group picture. Be sure to share these pictures in the children's rooms, too. This gives them a great sense of family identity.

Cowbell

I have an old cowbell that is positioned by our kitchen door. Two minutes before a meal is to be served I go out and ring that bell very firmly. This is a signal to the members of the family that the food is ready. They have two minutes to get to the table.

How Pretty!

Let your children wear your old jewelry and dress up when they have playtime.

Sorry

Admit when you're wrong. Your family members know when you've blown it as well as you do.

Pet Names

As the children get older, don't drop those pet names, but just use them privately to avoid embarrassing the kids.

Those School Projects

Take and use those special clay vases that are brought home. Use them as flower vases or to hold paper clips.

I'm Like Dad

Lend your son a tie to wear on special occasions.

I Choose You

Tell your children how much you enjoy being their parents. Kids like to hear they are loved.

31

A Team Effort Starts at Home

*Make my joy complete by being
of the same mind, maintaining the same love,
united in spirit, intent on one purpose.*

Philippians 2:2, NASB

֍ —— ֍

Regardless of whether I speak in California, Texas, Florida, or Canada, I will always get at least one question over and over again: "How do I get my husband and children involved?" I believe that it is one of the most-asked questions regarding the family.

I have been very blessed over the years. Bob has always been very supportive. At one time we had five children under our roof and I was only 21 years old. In order for us to survive, we had to work together. I know that isn't always the case.

The Scriptures teach that we are to live in harmony, to live together in love as though we had only one mind and one spirit (Philippians 2:2). Another one of our key verses is found in Ephesians 5:21: "Honor Christ by submitting to each other." We have tried to make these two verses formulate our attitudes toward husband-wife relationships, the way we raise our children, how we manage our finances, how we do chores around the home, how we handle changes in our lives, and the type of food we cook and the nutrition we put into our bodies.

Attitude management begins at home. This is the key, regardless if we are a college student living in the dorm, a single adult living in an apartment, a married couple living in an apartment or a small home, or a retired person living in a condo or mobile home. Our goal is to have an attitude that allows us to live in love and in harmony with those around us.

A lady called last week from northern California, and she stated that being disorganized last year has cost her a lot of money. It seems that she couldn't pay to get her federal tax form completed by her tax accountant, so she decided she would not file her return for last year. However, this was a very unwise decision on her part. The IRS has attached her payroll check in the amount of 2000 dollars until she can furnish proof that she owes less taxes. She feels that she has lost favor with her boss because of the attachment, plus it has cost her more money to have her CPA write letters on her behalf. She was in tears when she talked and stated, "I've got to get organized this year." As a mom do you, too, find yourself crying out for help?

Some of the women at my seminars cry out that they are so involved in so many activities that they feel all alone and need to "rent a wife." These women share that they have very little cooperation from their husband and children. As women we usually can't "rent a wife." We are it.

A spirit of cooperation must exist if Mom is to survive in our marriages; each person must carry his or her part of the load. Aesop, in one of his tales, illustrates this point by having his three sons each bring him a stick. He asks each of his sons to break their sticks. With little trouble they quickly snap their sticks in two. After each son has broken his stick, Aesop takes one twig from each son and ties them together. Then he asks each son to break the combined twigs. As hard as they try, not one son could break the bundle of twigs. Aesop points out that this is the way it is when a family joins together. We become strong, but by ourselves we are much weaker. He encourages his sons to band together and be strong. That's what we must do as families—join together and be strong.

In the good old days, the family had to pitch in to get all the chores done around the farm. Through this involvement together, we had the opportunity to spend time in conversation and talk about ethics, values, morals, church, Sunday school lessons, and growing up. Parents and children would find themselves working side by side. However, now we find that we have to plan to dialogue together.

When our children were small, Bob would help with feeding the children, bathing them, dressing them, and reading bedtime stories. This was a great help to me and gave the children an opportunity to bond with Dad.

With patio building, laying bricks, planting, landscaping, and installing sprinklers, Bob always had the children underfoot where he could show them how to do the tasks. At one point Bob shared with our son, Brad, who was about six that he was sorry to always have Brad be the "gopher." Brad replied, "That's okay, Dad. That's what little boys are for."

Over the years Dad and the children were big helps in lightening my load. The children rotated and helped with taking out the trash, feeding the animals, cleaning the pool, sweeping up the leaves on the patio, and helping Dad with his chores. They were great at emptying the dishwasher, sorting the dirty clothes, doing the wash, cleaning their rooms, and setting and clearing the table.

When our daughter, Jennifer, first started to drive a car at 16, she was thrilled to do our shopping at the market, make bank deposits, and run many of our errands.

When company was coming, everyone would pitch in and get things done. The children would even help address our party invitations, lick postage stamps, take the letters to the mailbox, welcome our guests, take their wraps and purses, help with soft drinks, serve the food, and help clean up the dinner dishes. We have really learned to value our time together as a family.

Even with all the involvement with the children, Bob and I also value our time together as a couple. We realized that our children would grow up fast and leave the nest. We didn't want to one day look at each other and ask, "Who are you?"

We found a workable solution to our unique problems, needs, and circumstances. You cannot copy us, but you can assess your own needs, abilities, and desires in order to come up with a solution.

Women ask me, "What rules should I follow in keeping a clean, organized home?" I tell them that each family must determine how clean they want their home to be to meet their own needs. This book gives you some tools with which you can meet the home-management goals of your family.

Try not to measure your home-management standards by those of a friend or neighbor. Your family is unique and must establish that level based upon its own "lifestyle needs."

As a team, you will learn to distinguish between your wants and your needs. What Bob needed was sometimes more important than what I needed. Sometimes my needs came first. We had to be sensitive to each other's needs at the moment. Sometimes one partner's needs are more urgent than those of the other at that moment. Be willing to shift gears.

I receive a lot of letters from mothers and wives who have very untypical schedules from the ordinary, and they want suggestions on how to adapt their schedules for their uniqueness. I don't always answer in detail because I want families to work out their own solutions. I just try to encourage them to come together and talk about how they can adapt their schedule to accommodate the requirements of various members of their families.

If one partner needs to study in the afternoons and evenings because of morning classes, the other mate might have to find something to do to occupy the time and be out of the way during those study periods. Many times sleeping schedules are big considerations for the family. This is where the family must come together to make sure that each family member gets adequate sleep.

Cooperation is the key. If you set up a marriage to be in competition rather than cooperation, no one wins. Work out disagreements in a spirit of harmony, and work as a team in managing your home and family.

In our Working Woman's Seminars, Bob and I teach how to set goals and establish priorities. Couples need to plan their futures. Where are you going to be five years from now? Bob and I were challenged at a couples' retreat when our children were young to think about what we wanted them to be as teenagers. We had never thought that far into the future. But when we got home, we wrote several goals we had for our children. They became our guidelines for their future training. To this day, almost 30 years later, we write family goals between Christmas and New Year's for the next year. These become our new goals for the next year. They're not set in concrete, but they do create a starting point. Be flexible.

Visualize your family's lives five years into the future. What do you hope to be doing in your family regarding finances, career, spiritual growth, profession, education, recreation, and physical areas of your life? Long-term goals help you make short-term decisions. When you have defined your goals in life, it makes establishing priorities so much easier. It also helps you say "no" more quickly to many questionable opportunities that come your way.

What obstacles keep you from becoming what you want to be? How can you take these negatives and turn them into positives? Concentrate on your goals rather than on the negatives if you want to succeed. Try alternate plans to meeting your goals. Success is a progressive realization of worthwhile goals. In our present-day culture we have lost the virtue of patience. Wait upon the Lord! Strive for patience not only for yourself but for your family. Teach it wherever possible. It takes 21 days to develop new habits. Start today!

Family Conferences

As parents we knew we wanted family involvement in making plans, establishing activities, and dreaming about specific areas concerning the Barnes family. We knew we had to delegate responsibilities, but in order to do that we had to have input from the children.

We set up specific family time on a regular basis. This provided us with an opportunity for the whole family to participate—to review guidelines and rules, to discuss future events, and many times just to have fun.

In *Survival for Busy Women* (Harvest House Publishers), I have devoted a whole chapter to the Family Conference Time.[1] It outlines in detail how our family utilized this very important time. Of all the activities we did, the family time together proved most valuable in keeping good communications in our family. The children knew that their input counted when a decision was made. I can remember on one occasion that it was time to purchase a new family car. In our discussing the particulars, the children asked Dad if we could get a color other than blue. It seems as though our last two cars were blue. That input really helped Bob and me. When we went shopping, blue was not what we were looking for. It was time we changed colors, and the children helped us make that decision.

Another time when we moved from one home to another that was out of town, we had narrowed our selection down to two neighborhoods and two different styles of homes. As we prayed about this decision, our children helped sway our initial selection. They made a better decision than we did. Their input really helped us make wiser decisions. These and many more illustrations came about because we were a family who met and planned together.

The length of our meetings varied according to the agenda and the ages of the various children. We tried to make it short and to the point—never too long to bore the children. Sometimes after only 15 minutes we were having refreshments; other times the meeting lasted 30 minutes. On fun night at the roller skating rink or ice skating rink, horseback riding, having a wiener roast or beach party, we would not have any formal agenda—just time together as a family. Oh yes, we would discuss certain items while driving in the car to and from the event. This was a great opportunity to talk in an informal way about values, stress, school, teachers, dates, party invitations, or preparing for a test. These casual moments gave us a lot of insight into our children, and gave them an opportunity to know Mom and Dad better. Deuteronomy 6:7 gave us a guideline in this style of teaching. This Scripture says, "And you shall teach them diligently to your sons and shall talk of them when you . . . walk by the way and when you lie down and when you rise up" (NASB).

Use every opportunity to teach your children; casual moments are usually the very best times for the children to grasp important concepts that will stay with them all their lives.

We usually kept our Family Conference Time for just family members because many times we had items on the agenda that were just for the Barnes family. However, during the fun nights we would rotate and let our children invite a friend as their guest. A lot of close friendships were made during these outings, plus we had an opportunity to build into the lives of our children's friends.

Be flexible with your plans, but make it a top priority for everyone to be at the family meetings. Consistency is most important. If Mom or Dad often aren't there, then the children feel that it's not too important and they will not be as excited about these "memory moments."

Management of the Home

In the traditional family role, I believe the Scriptures are clear that the husband has the responsibility of leadership in the home. I have been very fortunate over the years because Bob has always searched out God's leading in his life. He has read, listened, studied, and talked about how he can be a more effective husband.

I realize that that's the ideal, and that a lot of families are struggling in this area. My encouragement to you as wives is to let your husband manage in the home. Yes, you may be able to do it faster and better, but he needs to be accepted in those areas.

I also know that many homes in America do not have a man in the home. The wife must assume the leadership role even if she doesn't want that added responsibility. A home must have leadership in order to survive.

Jay Adams, in his book *Christian Living in the Home*, gives an excellent explanation of the husband's role as the manager of the home:

> A good manager knows how to put other people to work. . . . He will be careful not to

neglect or destroy his wife's abilities. Rather, he will use them to the fullest. He does not consider her someone to be dragged along. Rather, he thinks of her as a useful, helpful and wonderful blessing from God. . . . A manager has an eye focused on all that is happening in his home, but he does not do everything himself. Instead he looks at the whole picture and keeps everything under control. He knows everything that is going on, how it is operating, and only when it is necessary to do so, steps in to change and to modify or in some way to help.[2]

Since God gave woman to man to be his helpmate, we must manage together as a team. What are some of the techniques that Bob and I used in managing our home?

Planning—Establish and write out your mission or purpose for life. What do you want to do as an individual and as a family? Let your lives make a statement to your community. Take a look at what's going on and plan for the future. You must communicate these plans to everyone in the family. Use these guidelines as a basis for guiding your family. Of course, God's Word is the original and final word for direction, but how are you going to live His words out? Plan a schedule and schedule a plan.

Organization—Once you have thought out your purpose and mission in life, then you will need to establish organizational procedures to help reach these goals. Your home, people, equipment, and finances must be organized in a way that will make it possible for your family to reach the goals and objectives you have set. (See our address on page 343 of this book to obtain a price list of materials that will help you with your organization.)

Harmony—We are to live in harmony together. We were not made to fight and use our energies in arguments. A home that is in harmony is much more fun to live in. Love wins out over bickering and fighting. I have found that the woman is the harmonizer of a family. Staying married requires the love and devotion of both a man and a woman, but it still seems to be the woman who pays close attention to the personal needs and feelings of the people in her home. In harmonious living, the object is to make the other person feel better. It requires paying a lot of attention to the other members of the family. This is a very important concept for each member who lives within the family. It is most difficult because harmonizing requires a willingness to surrender one's own ego to the needs of the other family members.

Home Climate—Treat each member of the family with fairness and respect. Develop an awareness of what each member of the family is doing and *praise them, praise them*. Self-respect is developed in the home and in the extended family. If you are fortunate enough to involve aunts, uncles, cousins, nieces, nephews, grandma, and grandpa, so much the better. Ephesians 4:29 encourages us to let no corrupt communication come out of our mouth. Our speech is to be "edifying" (to lift or build up). It is to provide grace to the hearer. As parents, Bob and I insisted that respect be given to each member of our family. It meant that Mom and Dad had to exhibit that same respect to each other as well as to all members of our family. We value creativity, initiative, and a job well done. We praise and reward those who do a job well. That has extended right over to our grandchildren: Christine, Chad, Bevan, and Bradley. We have cute little stickers that say, "I Was Caught Being Good," that we give them when they do something on their own. With no direction from us, they decide by themselves they need to help out. It might be dusting the furniture, helping load the dishwasher, pulling weeds, picking up leaves off the patio, etc. We make this a big deal. They know they have done a good job—above and beyond. If one child gets a sticker, the other grandchildren will want the opportunity to get their very own, too. In a short time they also will be doing something good. It's a great way to build pride in family members. At times we even give PaPa Bob a sticker when he does something good. He likes that, too!

Control—Periodic evaluations must be made to make sure that the family is staying on target. Mom and Dad can tell quickly if the family is on target. Many times the children would point out in our conference time certain areas that we needed to consider as a family. This is why the family needs to stay flexible and be willing to change course.

You might be saying, "This sure sounds like a lot of work!" You know it is. Family takes a lot of work. It is a very responsible job, and wimps need not apply. My Bob has expressed this commitment that families need to ponder:

- All marriages aren't happy; living together is tough.

- A good marriage is not a gift; it's an achievement by God's grace.

- Marriage is not for children; it takes guts and maturity.

- Marriage separates the men from the boys and the women from the girls.

- Marriage is tested daily by the ability to compromise.

- The survival of marriage can depend on being smart enough to know what's worth fighting about, making an issue of, or even mentioning.

- Marriage is giving, and more importantly, forgiving.

- With all its ups and downs, marriage is still God's best object lesson of Jesus and the church.

- Through submission to one another we can witness to the world that marriage does work and is still alive.

- Marriage is worth dying for. If we give it proper honor, we will be honored by our children, our families, our neighbors, our friends, and best of all, our Lord.[3]

I believe it is time for parents in America to take charge of their families and redeem them for the Lord. It is very obvious that the styles of the sixties, seventies, and eighties aren't working. As God-fearing parents, we need to make things happen on purpose. We are to act with conviction and responsibility. Each family has its unique circumstances to consider, but with two willing parents we can become a team and we can be proud of our family.

Someone asked Dr. James Dobson what he thought was the future of the American family. He answered that, for the most part, women were committed to marriage, family, and children for the long haul. How successful the family of the future will be, he said, depends upon the father and what part he plays in that unit. Dads have got to take control of the family's direction. Priorities have to be evaluated and new ones written.

If America is to be strong, its families must be strong. It all starts with our individual families—no matter what they look like.

Proper organization within the family is a beginning for making your joy complete by being of the same mind, maintaining the same love, united in spirit, intent on one purpose: to glorify our Lord, Jesus Christ.

My prayers are with you as you try a new beginning. Try not to be supermom. It is a very tiring and lonely road—one which leads to burnout, frustration, and disappointment. The team effort does start at home and provides rich blessings of self-respect, pride for a job well done, and a feeling of cooperation. You will notice that the whole family's attitude will change and will most definitely lighten your load as Mom.

32

The Love Basket

*May the Lord bring you into
an ever deeper understanding
of the love of God and of the patience
that comes from Christ.*

2 Thessalonians 3:5

❧ —— ❧

Love Basket can be used for those very special times when you want to say "I love you" in a different way. It can be filled with food for dinner at the beach or by a lake or stream, or it can be taken to a ball game, a concert, or the park. It can even be taken in your car on a love trip. It may be a surprise lunch or dinner in the backyard, in your bedroom, or under a tree, but be creative and use it to say "I love you."

What You'll Need

Here are the things you'll need in order to make a Love Basket. First of all, you'll need a basket with a handle, preferably a heavy-duty basket something like a picnic basket without a lid but having a nice sturdy handle. Then you'll need a tablecloth. It can be made from a piece of fabric or from a sheet. I generally cut the tablecloth about 45" square. You'll want to line the inside of your basket with this tablecloth, letting it drape over the sides so it looks real cute. I make these for wedding shower gifts, anniversary gifts, or bridal gifts.

Inside our basket we're going to put two fancy glasses with a stem. It's nice to use glasses with tall stems so they look pretty in the basket. We'll also need four napkins. I like to use ones with a small print, or maybe a gingham, to make the basket look fun and different. One napkin will be for the lap and the other will be used as a napkin, but for now fluff up your napkins inside the top of the glasses so they puff up and look like powder puffs inside your pretty glasses.

Next you'll need to add a nice tall candle holder and a candle. I like to use something tall because it shows over the top of the basket. You'll also need a bottle of sparkling apple cider. This is nonalcoholic, but it bubbles up very nicely. (You can buy this in the juice department of your market.) You'll want a loaf of French bread, plus some pretty fresh flowers to make the basket look really fun and inviting. Also, you'll want some cheese, salami, dill pickles, and any other good things that you really like.

Love Basket Ideas

Now let me share with you some ideas I have for my Love Basket. I've been making Love Baskets for my husband for over 40 years. We all sense times when our husband needs a little extra attention. Maybe things have been tough at work, or maybe he's depressed over something, or maybe he just needs to feel that he's needed. Maybe you've had things out of priority, and you need to get things back into priority and to let him know that he's important in your life. These are times when you want to put together a Love Basket.

I can remember saying to my friend or neighbor, "You know, my Bob needs a Love Basket tomorrow night, and I'd like to do it for him. Would you take the kids for a few hours for me? The next time your husband needs a Love

Basket, I'll take your kids for you." I'll tell you, they're happy to do it for you. And I'm happy to do it for anyone.

This last Valentine's Day we had a Love Basket even though the kids are grown up now. Bob and I weren't going to be able to be together on Valentine's Day, so I decided I would make a Love Basket for him the night before. That morning I called him at work and said, "Tonight I want to take you out to a special restaurant that you've never been to before that has your very favorite food." He asked, "Well, where is it?" I replied, "I'm not going to tell you. It's just a special place in town that I'm going to take you tonight. Could you be home by six o'clock?" Do you know what? He got home at 5:30!

What he didn't know was that during the morning I had fried up his very favorite Southern fried chicken. I had also made potato salad, fruit salad, and some yummy rolls. I had the whole dinner prepared in the morning because I didn't want the house to smell from food and give away the surprise when he walked in the door that night.

Dinner on the Deck

At that time we lived in a two-story house with a deck off our bedroom that overlooked the city, with a beautiful view of everything. We had never had dinner on our deck before, so I took a card table up there, plus a couple of folding chairs. I put the red-and-white gingham tablecloth on the table, as well as the candleholder and a red candle. I put the special red plate on his side of the table. I put a beautiful Valentine card right on the plate for him, lit a candle in our bedroom, and had the music all ready to turn on. It was the most beautiful restaurant in town. It was just gorgeous that night.

Bob came in. "Well, where are we going?" he asked. I replied, "It's a surprise." He asked, "Do I have to change my clothes or anything?" I said, "No, you're perfect just the way you are." So I went into the kitchen and picked up the Love Basket. (In the Love Basket were all his favorite foods covered with the cloth). I handed him the Love Basket and said, "Follow me." Bob knows now, after 40 years, that when the Love Basket comes out, really special things are going to happen. So he followed me eagerly.

We went upstairs where the candle was lit and the music going. As he walked out onto the deck, he saw that beautiful tablecloth with the candle and the red plate and the glasses and the napkins. He opened the Love Basket and took out the fried chicken plus all the other special things. That evening we had a beautiful meal together enjoying each other, communicating with each other, and loving each other.

Now what was I telling Bob by doing this? I was telling him that I loved him, that he was important, that I cared for him. I didn't have to tell him all I had done that day to prepare for our evening. He knew I took the time to set the table, to make it special. He knew I had worked hard to make that dinner very special to him. Do you know what he felt like? He felt like a king. He knew that he was the top priority in my life.

Jenny's Love Basket

Let me tell you a fun experience that Jenny had. She made a breakfast Love Basket for Craig when they were courting. I'll never forget the morning they were going to Los Angeles for the whole day for a dental convention. Jenny put a Love Basket together with flowers, candles, candelabra, orange juice, bran muffins, fresh strawberries, and sliced cantaloupe. When Craig came to pick her up at 6 A.M., he couldn't believe his eyes. He'd never seen anything like that before, especially at 6 A.M.! Later Jenny said, "Mom, it was so great. We got in the car and I did everything. I put the napkin on his lap and we ate on the freeway and had our little Love Basket together." This is a sure way to get a husband. At least it worked for Jenny, because five months later they were married!

Craig's Love Basket

One year later, our son-in-law, Craig, made a Love Basket for their first anniversary. He wanted it to be a surprise, so he put it all together with special hors d'oeuvres and hid it in the car. When Jenny came home from work, he told her they needed to run a few errands. What she didn't know was that he was organized. He had planned a Love Basket over the cliffs of Corona del Mar with crashing waves below, just one hour from their home. He also had made reservations for their one-year anniversary night in a hotel in Laguna Beach.

They enjoyed their Love Basket. To Jenny's surprise, Craig had candlelight, napkins, cloth, and all. It was perfect. He then whisked her away to the hotel. When she discovered what he was doing she exclaimed, "Craig, I can't stay overnight. I have no clothes." Craig had taken care of that too. He had her clothes, beach towel, lounge chair, bathing suit, and all. However, when he got to her makeup he wasn't sure just what to bring, so you know what he did? He took out her whole makeup drawer and put it into the car. Can't you see them carrying the drawer into the hotel? But who cares—it was a way of showing his love to her.

A Letter of Love

Let me share with you two letters I have received from two women who have attended my seminars.

Dear Emilie:

I'm still thinking about your seminar and how much food for thought you offered. Everyone had to go away with treasures in thought, word, or deed. From your testimony to your organizing and all the helpful hints, I thank you. And the Love Basket—well, that was the best of them all.

Just ask my husband. He got his first one Saturday night. He absolutely loved it, sparkling apple cider and all. Candlelight. He was so thrilled that he says he'll have to thank you personally for that one. It was so much fun that we even had ours in our bedroom. You helped me so much by just one statement you made about seeking and having the quiet and gentle spirit. God used you that night and answered my prayer for help concerning how to deal and communicate with my son. I was getting all worked up and frustrated and was arguing with him. Now I'm firm, gentle, and quiet, and it works. Thank You, Lord, and thank you, Emilie. I thought you'd like to hear that one because I want to encourage you to go on with your ministry, as it's blessing lives.

Love,
Rosemary

Dear Emilie:

I've so much wanted to write and share with you. This has been on my heart for a long time.

I have always been a very proud person. So, in my relationship with my husband, I would never give my all. I guess I feared he would make fun of me or use me. I was very cold. I never said or did nice things for him.

In your seminar you shared with us about the "Love Basket." It touched my heart. I talked with you after the seminar and shared with you that my husband had cancer. You said you would pray for us. Thank you for your prayers.

I decided to buy a basket and give my husband a "Love Basket." I went all out. I decorated and made a special meal. It was around Valentine's Day so I had a red tablecloth. I bought him a little present. He worked nights and came home at 12:30 A.M. I told him I had a surprise for him when he came home. I really fixed myself up for him, set my hair, and fixed my makeup. (He liked that. . . . I had always been a slob at home.) When he walked in, he saw the table and the candlelight. I greeted him with a kiss. We had a wonderful time. He told me it was the nicest thing I had ever done for him. I'll cherish that time forever.

My husband died a month later. I pray that if you share this letter with the ladies you speak to, it might touch someone's heart like mine had been touched. Set aside your pride and give to your loved ones.

A Friend in Christ,
Denise

33

Plan a Picnic

And why worry about your clothes?
Look at the field lilies!
They don't worry about theirs.

Matthew 6:28

ࠥ —— ࠥ

What you do today is what you and your family will remember tomorrow. As mothers we want to purposefully plan to build warm memories to create those "special moments" that add to the foundation of a warm, functioning family. Over the years we have created memories through wonderful picnics.

Fun-filled memories of special family times can happen by taking a picnic meal to the park, lake, beach, mountains, desert, backyard, or to any favorite picnic areas.

Many of our best picnics have been spur-of-the-moment, last-minute decisions based upon the weather or a change in our schedule. However, with the hurried lifestyle we all have, you may want to think ahead and reserve the time on your calendar.

Don't feel that you always have to have excellent weather. Some of our fun times and special memories have occurred when the weather hasn't always been its best: an unexpected rain, high winds, dust storms, rough waves at the beach.

While it's always nice to plan and prepare ahead, many times the best outings are the "Let's Have a Picnic" picnic—a quick raid on the refrigerator and cupboard and off you go to some pleasant spot under a shady tree. A good tuna sandwich, some pickles, fruit, and an icy drink will always taste good outdoors.

I was four years old when my family took a picnic lunch to the desert under a yucca tree. The setting doesn't sound real exciting, but I can still remember the green-and-white checkered tablecloth my mother pulled out and spread on the sand. From an old basket, Mom pulled plates, glasses, plastic ware, and some delicious food. She took me by the hand and we picked a few wild-flowers for the centerpiece. After lunch we all took a nature walk and collected fun memories. My brother and I still talk about that first picnic, and that was over 45 years ago. What lasting memories!

Picnics are for everyone and loved by everyone around the world and can be planned for any time of the year. Our early-American picnics were called "frolics" and consisted of games, music, flirtations, and plenty of good food. Join together with another family or several single-adult families and create a theme for the special occasion.

Depending upon your geographic location and the time of year, you might want to consider:

- *Mardi Gras Feast*—chicken gumbo, steamed rice, marinated green beans, and New Orleans King Cake.

- *Abalone Steak Picnic*—fried catfish, hush puppies, tomato slices, and lemon tarts.

- *New England Clam Bake*—baked clams, Boston baked beans, brown bread, hot cider, and melon slices.

- *Hawaiian Luau*—glazed chicken wings, rice salad, coconut fruit, and Hawaiian punch.

- *A Vermont Snow Snack*—navy bean soup, stuffed baked potatoes, hot cocoa, and maple cupcakes.

- *San Francisco Crab Lunch*—cracked crab, leafy salad, sourdough bread, and chocolate cake.

- *Indian Summer Brunch*—cucumber salad, squaw bread, and smoked salmon.

- *Midwest Corn Feed*—barbecued corn, vegetable cheese bake, whole wheat bread, and apple pie with homemade ice cream.

- *Pumpkin Patch Picnic*—hot pumpkin soup, apple spice cake, and hot wassail cider.

- *Thanksgiving Dinner*—smoked turkey or roast duck, stuffed acorn squash, and spicy pumpkin bread.

- *Plantation Buffet*—Ham with orange glaze, candied yams, melon balls, pecan pie, and minted iced tea.

- *Sundae Stop*—variety of homemade ice cream with 15 different toppings, from nuts to cookie crumbs and sauces.

- *Mexican Memories*—taco salad, tortillas, iced lemon-limeade.

- *All-American Apple Pie Picnic*—fried chicken, biscuits and honey, black-eyed pea salad, cold watermelon, and apple pie with cheese.

These are just a few theme ideas. You can develop your own themes and recipes for each picnic.

After you have made the decision to have a picnic, decided on the theme, selected and prepared the food, you have to decide how you are going to keep your foods cold.

Keeping Foods Cold

- The length of time in which food can spoil is relative to the temperature outdoors and to the way the food was cooked, chilled, wrapped, and carried. Foods containing mayonnaise, eggs, cream, sour cream, yogurt, or fish are safe unrefrigerated up to two hours *if the weather is fairly cool*. If it will be more than two hours before you eat, plan to carry along a refrigerated cooler. Cool dishes as quickly as possible after preparing them and leave them in the refrigerator until just before time to leave.

- Remember this cardinal rule: *Never take anything on a picnic that could possibly spoil unless you can provide effective portable refrigeration.*

- Ice chests or coolers can be chilled with ice cubes, crushed or chipped ice, blocks from ice machines, or water frozen in clean milk cartons or other containers.

- Fill plastic bottles (with lids) two-thirds full with water to allow for expansion and freeze them overnight. These frozen containers eliminate the mess of melted ice. Fruit juice in plastic bottles can also be frozen ahead and used in the cooler. Juice will thaw readily when needed.

- Dry ice may also be used in coolers. Place it on top of foods so that the chilling carbon dioxide, heavier than air, travels downward. Wrap dry ice in several layers of paper; never place it unwrapped in the cooler.

- Permanently sealed refrigerator blocks are very handy. They are several degrees colder than ice, can be kept in the freezer between picnics, and don't melt as ice does.

- Store cold drinks on the bottom with foods on top or in a separate compartment if the cooler is divided.

- You can count on heavily insulated metal coolers to keep food sufficiently cold from 24 to 48 hours. Inexpensive Styrofoam coolers work well for much shorter periods, depending on the weather and the amount of ice. Open all ice chests as little as possible after filling. Never allow coolers to stand open. Find a shady place for the cooler during the picnic and cover it with a blanket, beach towels, or a canvas tarpaulin.

- It's a good idea to transport mayonnaise in small containers in an ice chest; then add the mayonnaise to salads or spread on sandwiches at the picnic site.

- Whipped cream can be transported in a sealed plastic jar or bowl in the cooler; or take a wire whisk to whip the cream at the picnic.

- Combine rinsed, dried, torn, and chilled salad greens in a plastic bowl or bag that seals; keep chilled in cooler. Carry dressing in a separate container and toss salad at the last minute. Pack watercress, parsley, mint, grapes, lemon slices and other garnishes in sealed bags for finishing dishes on-site.

- Add cold foods or liquids to thermoses that have been chilled with ice water or placed in the refrigerator for an hour. Food will stay cold from several hours to all day, depending on the weather and how often you open the container.

Packing, Transporting, and Safe-Storing Tips

In packing food to go you might want to:

- Prepare all food as close to departure time as comfortably possible for you. Don't cook something earlier than the time recommended in the recipe, unless the item can be frozen successfully.

- Whenever possible, pack your hamper or other carryall in reverse order from the way in which you'll use the items at the site: food on the bottom, then serving items and tableware, finally the tablecloth on top.

- Always place food containers right side up to prevent spills and breakage. Leaking foods can ruin everything in the hamper. If tops of containers do not fit securely, reinforce them with a band of masking tape around the lid. Play it very safe and put jars or bowls that might leak inside heavy-duty plastic bags and secure the top of the bag with tape, twist-ties, or rubber bands.

- Breakable glassware can be wrapped in the tablecloth, napkins, kitchen towels, paper towels, or newspaper. Separate breakable items with plastic containers or soft goods when filling the hamper. Wrap fragile items well and place in a separate container to be held while traveling.

- Foods such as pies, tarts, cakes, muffins, mousses, molded salads, or homebaked breads that crumble easily can be carried in the pans in which they were prepared. At time of baking, cakes and bread are turned out to cool, then slipped back into their pans and wrapped in foil for protection en route. Coffee cans are handy to bake in and easy to carry. At the picnic, just open the bottom

of the can with a can opener and push out the
bread or cake.

- Use masking tape to hold springform pans (with
removable bottoms) in place while traveling. Consider carrying along the frosting separately for
simple cakes baked in flat pans. Frost at the picnic
site.

- Don't leave vacant spots in the picnic hamper or
box. If the supplies do not fill the container, fill in
with rolled newspaper or paper towels to prevent
foods from overturning or bumping together.

Bags

Shopping bags are excellent for holding everything
for a simple picnic. In New York it's quite chic to be seen
with a famous West Side deli bag packed with food. Save
attractive shopping bags for transporting excess items
that won't fit into the main picnic hamper. Brown-paper
market bags make wonderful carryalls. If the item you
plan to carry is heavy, you may want to double your bags
(place one inside the other) to give added strength. Children may want to decorate these bags to add a flair to
them—it's a good activity to channel some of their
excess energies. With some care, these bags can be
reused several times.

Baskets

Wicker baskets or hampers are the traditional picnic
carryalls. However, anything goes these days. Import
shops sell baskets made in many different shapes, sizes,
and price ranges.

Plastic carriers, totes, canvas packs, and duffel bags all
make great picnic baskets. Cartons, boxes, and chests
can be used, too.

The important part is the time spent with your family and friends sharing your love together.

Ground Covers and Tablecloths

Choose a blanket, patchwork quilt, bedspread, sheet, comforter, afghan, woolen throw, or any large piece of fabric for a ground cover or tablecloth. Top it, if you like, with a decorative second cloth that fits the mood of the picnic you've planned.

No-iron cotton or synthetic fabric is easy to keep clean and ready for traveling. Other choices to consider are beach towels, bamboo or reed matting, nylon parachute fabric, flannel shirt material, or lengths of any easy-care fabric stitched at each end.

Purchase one or two plastic painter's drop cloths or carry a canvas tarpaulin to put down before you spread the tablecloth if the ground is damp, dusty, or snow-covered.

Top off the setting with a centerpiece made by the children from resources taken from the area. This might include flowers, shells, wood, nuts, and rocks found nearby. This also gives you an opportunity to take a nature walk before food time. If your children show a special interest in what they find, you might want to follow up at your local library. This picnic might become the stimulus for a new hobby.

Additional Super Picnic Ideas

- *A Cooking Contest:* Let the various members of your family or invited guests bake their favorite recipe. Vote for your favorite and award special ribbons or prizes.

- *Winter Picnic Indoors:* Cover tables with red-and-white checkered cloths; set out salads, finger foods, and a basket of breads, plus plastic utensils and paper goods. Enjoy a carefree picnic indoors.

- *A Birthday That's Not for Kids Only:* So it's Billy's big day again. This time invite his friends' parents, too. Two parties are better than one. One parent handles the children and the other parent hosts the grown-ups; then switch halfway through.

- *The Four-Part Picnic Party:* Traveling in a group of four couples, have hors d'oeuvres at one home, salads at the next, the entrée at another, and the dessert at the last. Idea: Collect recipes and make cookbooks for everyone.

- *The Impromptu Picnic:* Call up some friends in the afternoon and pick up a party on the way to the picnic area. Stop for chicken, fast food, drinks, dips, and chips.

- *Going Fishing:* All aboard! Rent a boat for the day and invite some friends along. Each person can bring his or her own food; or, for a small contribution by each person, one person can make the food and bring it along. It's a lot of fun even if only a few fish are caught.

- *A Block Party:* Have one section of your neighborhood or one floor of your apartment supply appetizers, have another bring main dishes, and another bring desserts.

- *Potluck Picnic:* Don't forget this favorite old-fashioned way to get to know neighbors and to try out new recipes, too. Ask people to bring their best dishes to this picnic.

🍒 PICNIC PLANNING CHECKLIST 🍒

In the Refrigerator
- ☑ Beverages
- ☐ Breads/muffins
- ☐ Butter/margarine
- ☐ Catsup/Worchestershire sauce
- ☐ Cheeses/spreads
- ☐ Eggs
- ☑ Fruit
- ☐ Lemons and limes
- ☐ Meats
- ☐ Milk/cream
- ☐ Mustard/mayonnaise
- ☐ Pickles/olives
- ☑ Relishes
- ☐ Salad makings/sandwich garnishes
- ☐ Vegetables
- ☑ Sparkling apple cider

In the Freezer
- ☐ Breads
- ☐ Cakes/cookies
- ☐ Cheeses
- ☐ Chopped Onions/peppers
- ☑ Coffee (decaffeinated)
- ☐ Homemade broths/soups
- ☑ Ice
- ☐ Pie Crusts
- ☐ Sandwiches (w/o mayonnaise or lettuce)
- ☐ Vegetables

On the Shelves
- ☑ Beverages
- ☐ Canned brown bread and nut bread
- ☐ Canned fish
- ☐ Canned meats
- ☐ Canned soups and broths
- ☐ Canned vegetables
- ☑ Chocolate chips/candies
- ☐ Chips
- ☐ Crackers
- ☐ Cookies
- ☐ Dried Fruits
- ☐ Garlic Salt
- ☐ Herbs/spices
- ☐ Marinated artichoke hearts

On the Shelves (continued)
- ☐ Powdered milk
- ☑ Nuts/trail mix snacks
- ☐ Olive Oil/salad oil
- ☐ Olives
- ☐ Onions/garlic
- ☑ Peanut butter
- ☐ Pimentos/peppers
- ☐ Salt and pepper
- ☐ Sugar/honey
- ☐ Vinegar

Equipment
- ☑ Athletic equipment
- ☐ Basket, hamper/tote
- ☑ Can/bottle opener
- ☑ Charcoal (self starting)
- ☐ Coffee creamer
- ☐ Cups: plastic, insulated
- ☐ First-aid kit
- ☑ Flashlight
- ☐ Flatware: plastic or stainless steel
- ☐ Folding stove/hibachi
- ☐ Folding table
- ☐ Fuel/matches
- ☑ Games
- ☐ Glasses: plastic or glass
- ☐ Insect repellant
- ☐ Knives
- ☐ Mess kits/plastic or metal
- ☐ Moist towelettes
- ☐ Napkins: paper or cloth
- ☑ Paper towels
- ☐ Plastic/canvas groundcloth
- ☐ Plastic food containers/wraps or bags
- ☑ Plates: paper or plastic
- ☐ Portable seating: folding chairs or stools
- ☑ Serving spoons
- ☐ Tablecloth
- ☐ Temporary shelter/shade
- ☐ Thermoses, cooler/ice chest
- ☑ Trash bags
- ☐ Tupperware containers
- ☑ Vase or jar for flowers

34

Creative Entertaining

Don't forget to be kind to strangers,
for some who have done this
have entertained angels
without realizing it!

Hebrews 13:2

❧ —— ❧

Something I discovered not too many years ago was the idea of using sheets as tablecloths and napkins. One of the things that's great about using sheets is that you get lots of fabric for a modest amount of money, plus they're all wash-and-wear. You can wash them, throw them into the dryer, and put them right back onto the table. So throw away the plastic cloth you've wiped off for years, and get into sheets!

If you're going to be married or want to buy a new set of dishes, you might want to buy just a plain set of white or bone dishes. They will go with any kind of tablecloth, or anything else you choose. We can't all go out and do that, so we may have to do with what we have. My everyday dishes happen to be brown-and-white calico. I started looking for sheets that would go with my brown-and-white dishes, and I had a lot of fun doing this. One set I bought in the basement of a department store. The sheets have a little border on the bottom and some black and white and brown on the top.

Using What We Have

Now you say, "Well, Emilie, you've got a border on the bottom of the sheet. Don't you cut off the border? You only have one border on a sheet." No, I don't cut off the border. I place the sheet so that the border shows on the most obvious end of the table. This way, as you walk into my dining room or family room you see the sheet on the table with the border showing. Nobody has ever come into my home and run around to the other side of the table to see if there's a border over there.

I took the bottom sheet (the fitted sheet), which happened to be a print, and made napkins out of it. Then for a napkin holder I used a small star-shaped cookie cutter. With some white daisies on the table, I have a pretty table setting at very low cost.

For a napkin holder you might try using one of those big fat paper clips that you can buy in a stationery store. They come in all kinds of different bright colors, and they make great little gifts.

Placemats

Placemats are another nice thing to have. You can make them out of quilted fabric. A yard-and-a-half of fabric will make four placemats. Double up the quilted fabric and put the two right sides together. Cut each 14" x 22", then sew it all the way around except for about 4" at the top for a little opening. Then reverse it, and tuck in the top where the opening was. Stitch it all the way around two times to get a double stitching. (That makes it stay nice and flat. It's a little heavier on the edges and stays firm on the table.) These placements can go in the washing machine, in the dryer, and back on the table.

The Red Plate

One December my Bible study group completed the year with a salad luncheon. We finished early in the month so the women could have time to prepare for the holiday and spend time with their families.

The women presented me, their teacher, with one of the best gifts I've ever received. It was a red plate with beautiful white lettering surrounding the outside which says "You Are Special Today." My heart felt warm and so very special. They were expressing their thanks and love through this unique gift. As we shared each other's salads that day, I ate off the special red plate.

I discovered that the plate was hand-glazed of fine ceramic and is like no other plate. No two are exactly alike, even though a company makes them. I was now the owner of an original red plate!

Knowing the feeling I received using the red plate, I wanted to share that same feeling with other people. As Christmas drew near, my beautiful turkey dinner was in preparation. That Christmas day was warm and cozy, with the smell of pine and roasting turkey. Our family of 26 gathered around the buffet table for a time of praise and thanksgiving. Now was the time to present the red plate to some special person in our family.

My Bob and I chose the most special person who came into our lives and family that year. Our daughter, Jenny, was married that September, and Craig, her new husband and our son-in-law, was the most special gift of God to us as a family. He was number one, as it was his first Christmas with us. I wish you could have seen his eyes and the cute smile that crossed his face when we announced that he was the one who got to eat Christmas dinner off the "You Are Special Today" red plate.

More Happiness

Our red plate use didn't end there. As I mentioned in chapter 32, as February came along, I planned a special dinner for my husband to celebrate Valentine's Day. I made a "Love Basket," filled with his favorite foods, and we had dinner on our patio, located outside our bedroom.

The card table I set up looked beautiful with a red-and-white gingham cloth, white eyelet napkins, candle, flowers, and at Bob's place the red plate saying "You Are Special Today." I knew he was making his choice of who would be his special Valentine, and I wanted to be the one! At the sight of the table with the plate, all so simple, yet so beautiful, my Bob expressed his love and thanks for making him feel like he was my number-one man. It was another way of telling him I loved him and appreciated all he did for our family.

I then discovered that our red plate was an American tradition that the early American families used when someone deserved special praise or attention. God tells us in His Word that we are to encourage each other and build each other up (1 Thessalonians 5:11). Now, generations later, we can return to this custom and use it to feed on the positive. I continue to remind my Bible study women to tell *God* the negative about their husband and family, and tell the *person* the positive. Now we had another way to express that positive attitude.

When our son, Brad, turned 21, we had a family dinner to celebrate this special year. As he sat down at his place, there sat the red plate, another way of telling him, "We're proud of you. We're proud that God gave us a son, and now you're a man. Bless you, our son, as you meet life with God's hand on yours."

By now we had purchased a special pen that writes on ceramic and won't wash off. So we began to list on the back of the plate the dates and special occasions it was used for. As the years pass we will always have the remembrance of all the special times and dates.

This year Bob and I discipled and counseled two special young women. They wanted to do something special for Bob, as his birthday was drawing near, so they invited both of us out for lunch. I took the red plate along, hidden in my tote bag, and asked the waitress to serve Bob his lunch off the "You Are Special Today" plate. What a surprise when the red plate appeared in the restaurant with lunch served on it! The chef was chuckling along with all the other people that day as they watched him receive his lunch. Did he feel special? You bet!

Building the Good

I'm more excited than ever to build the positive and good self-esteem into others with this plate. Our plate was priceless by now and becoming a family heirloom, one we can hand down from generation to generation, especially with all the occasions and dates listed on the back.

I suggested to a mother, who was in a dilemma as to what to give her son's teacher at the end of the school year, the possibility of collecting 50 cents per child from the class and purchasing a "You Are Special Today" plate (with pen) and having all the children sign and date the back. "Great idea!" she exclaimed, and did so. As she related the opening of the gift, her eyes filled with joy as the teacher read the beautiful lettering: "You Are Special Today," and hugged the plate.

In my husband's family there are three sons: Bob, his twin brother, Bill, and younger brother, Ken. Their birthdays all fall in the same month, a day apart. Bob's mother, Gertie, always makes a big celebration for their birthdays. I wanted to take the red plate along, again hidden in my tote bag, but I didn't have three plates. So, thinking of a creative way to use the plate, I decided it was natural to use it for Gertie! After our blessing I took Mom Gertie's hands and thanked her for her love and warmth over the years. What a special lady to have given us three daughters-in-law such wonderful husbands! We expressed our thanks for her time and love to all our children (her 14 grandchildren). There was no doubt that she was the one that day to experience the magic of the red plate.

By now I'm sure you're seeing the excitement of using a plate to speak volumes of love when many times words aren't enough. Other ideas for the plate could be a job promotion, homecoming, when an old friend visits, good report card, new baby, graduation, engagement, Father's Day, anniversary, Mother's Day, winning the big game, and many others.

God bless you as you build up the positive in other people.

35

How to Give a Piggy Party

*I will give you a new heart—I will
give you new and right desires—and
put a new spirit within you.*

Ezekiel 36:26

❧ —— ❧

piggy party is basically a party with a theme.
You want to make it as much fun as you possibly
can, not only for yourself but also for your
guests. To get started you'll need the proper materials.
You'll need a pink sheet or pink tablecloth (or you could
take a white sheet and dye it pink). You'll also want to get
matching pink napkins.

Your invitations can be made up on brown construction paper. Take grocery bags and cut them open to show
the inside—just plain brown paper. Don't use anything
really nice and fancy, because that's not the way piggies
are. Then buy some pink piggy stickers (or make them
from pink construction paper), and put the piggies on
your invitations. Do the same thing for your name tags.
You may also want to buy an apron with pigs on it or else
make your own piggy apron.

You'll want everybody to wear pink. That should be a
necessity. When you send out the invitations, have them
read: "Please wear pink." Have some pink shirts handy
in case somebody decides to come to your party without

wearing pink. You could also make some type of pink piggy hats for your guests.

MENU

Pink Ripple Punch Cocktail

* * *

Greens and Hog Rind (Spinach Salad)

* * *

Porky Bread (Corn Bread)

* * *

Sausage Slop

* * *

Mud Pie

* * *

Leftover Coffee and Tea

(All recipes serve 8-12 guests)

Pink Ripple Punch Cocktail

Mix one part 7-Up with one part cranberry juice cocktail. Add lots of ice and a sprig of mint, if available.

Greens and Hog Rind

1 or 2 bunches spinach—clean, rinse, and spin out
1/4 lb. mushrooms, sliced thin
bacon bits (fresh or in the jar)
1 cup bean sprouts
sliced red onion
2 hard-boiled eggs, grated or chopped
bottle of Lawry's Canadian Bacon Salad Dressing (or Italian dressing)

In a large bowl place greens. Add bean sprouts, onion, mushrooms, hard-boiled eggs, and bacon bits. Toss with salad dressing.

Porky Bread

1 cup fresh cornmeal
1 cup whole wheat flour (can be white)
1 egg
4 tsp. baking powder
1 tsp. salt
1/4 cup honey
1/4 cup oil
1 cup milk

Mix and bake in a greased square pan at 425° for 20-30 minutes.

Sausage Slop

12 hot Italian sausages
 2 or more sliced yellow squashes
 3 or more sliced summer squashes
 1 eggplant—peel and dice into medium pieces
 1 lb. fresh mushrooms (quartered)
 2 green peppers—cut into medium pieces

2 zucchini, sliced
2 large cans of whole tomatoes

Leave sausages whole and brown very well in a skillet. In a large pot, put all other ingredients with the two cans of whole tomatoes. Add seasonings and sausage (garlic salt; Lawry's Seasoned Salt). Bring to a boil and simmer two to three hours. Serve in large bowls with one to two sausages per person. Oink, oink good! Serves 10-12.

Mud Pie

1/2 package Nabisco chocolate wafers
1/2 cube butter, melted
1 quart coffee ice cream
1 1/2 cups fudge sauce
Whipped cream
Slivered almonds

Crush wafers and add butter; mix well. Press into 9" pie plate. Cover with softened coffee ice cream. Put into freezer until ice cream is firm. Top with cold fudge sauce (it helps to place pie in freezer for a time to make spreading easier). Store in freezer approximately 10 hours. Slice mud pie into 8-12 portions and serve on a chilled dessert plate with a chilled fork. Top with whipped cream and slivered almonds.

(Recipe compliments of "The Chart House" Restaurant.)

Centerpiece

leafy spinach
red leaf lettuce
cabbage
corn-on-the-cob (if available)
radishes with tops
mushrooms
carrots with tops

green onions
bamboo skewers
9" x 13" Pyrex dish or flat-type basket

Food and Fun

Your centerpiece should be made up of things that pigs like. This is a fun opportunity to show your creativity. Every time you make the centerpiece it could turn out a little different. You need a basket, plus a Pyrex dish or bowl to put inside the basket, plus two inches of water inside the bowl to keep the vegetables fresh. You'll also need some long bamboo skewers. (You can buy them in the market.) A head of cabbage is placed first on the bottom of the bowl. Lettuce greens go around the inside edges of the basket. (You might also use parsley, spinach, turnips, carrots with greens left on, etc.— anything leafy that pigs like.) Into your basic head of cabbage or lettuce should go skewers topped with carrots, radishes, mushrooms, brussels sprouts, green peppers, tomatoes, etc.

If you're going to have a potluck, take the recipes provided in this book and make them available to the people who are bringing food (so that everybody has the same menus). For instance, if you're going to have Pink Ripple Punch Cocktail, have some people bring the 7-Up and other people bring the cranberry juice. You provide the ice and the punch bowl.

Sausage Slop is your main dish, and it is absolutely delicious. It's very simple to make, too. It just has the sausage and a lot of vegetables. Don't leave anything out that's shown on the recipe—it's all important.

You won't believe how cute your party looks when everyone wears pink. All your guests will think it's a great idea, and they'll probably even want to do piggy parties of their own.

But the most important thing in all this is not just to be able to put on a well-organized piggy party, but to become the organized and creative woman that God wants you to be. He wants you to be touched by the power of the Holy Spirit as you minister Christ to other people. As Jesus said in Matthew 6:33 (KJV), "Seek ye first the kingdom of God, and his righteousness; and all these things shall be added unto you."

HOW TO GIVE A PIGGY PARTY

Materials Needed

Tablecloth:	A pink sheet or a printed pink sheet or a white sheet you can dye pink.
Napkins:	Matching the cloth or paper napkins with pigs on them.
Invitations:	Dirty beige construction paper and piggy stickers.
Name tags:	Dirty beige construction paper and piggy stickers.
Menu:	Provided.
Centerpiece:	Lots of greens and vegetables.

PLEASE WEAR PINK!

**YOU'RE INVITED
TO A
PINK PIGGY PARTY**

COME DRESSED IN PINK

When: February 27
Slop Time: 6:00 P.M.
Pigpen: Barnes' Barn
RSVP: Regrets only!
*We're going to have
an Oink of a time!*

PIGGY GAME INSTRUCTIONS

Equipment Needed

1. Enough tables and chairs for a multiple of 4-6 players at each table.
2. Pen or pencil for each player.
3. One die for each table.
4. One pink game sheet for each player.

Objective

To roll the die and be the first person to draw the pig with all its parts. When this is done, the person with the completed pig yells out *Piggy!* This constitutes the end of the game.

Directions

1. By looking at the game sheet, you will notice that the pig has a body, a head, two ears, two eyes, a tail, and four legs.
2. Each of the parts may be drawn by the proper roll of the die. In order to draw the body for each game, the player must roll a (1) first. After the body is drawn, you may add tail and legs, but you must roll a (2) for the head before you can draw the ears (3) or eyes (4).
3. To determine who starts the roll for each game at each table, each player at each table rolls the die. The player with the highest number on the die is first to roll when the game begins.
4. When all players are ready to roll the die, the host or hostess will call out, "*Oink, oink.*" The game begins.
5. In a clockwise direction, each player rolls the die until he or she has a (1) on the die. Then they draw the

shape of the pig's body on the space given for that game.

6. You may not draw any other parts of the pig's anatomy until the body has been drawn. However, you may draw the tail and legs before you have the head drawn.

7. After the body is drawn, you must roll a (2) for the head before you can draw the ears (3) or eyes (4).

8. After the body has been drawn, the player gets a second roll if he/she rolls a (6).

9. The first player to complete all parts of the pig yells out *Piggy!* This completes the game. All players total their scores for the game (see the list of points for the various parts of the pig) and write the amount on the total line for that game. (If a person yells *Piggy!* and doesn't have all the parts drawn, ten points are deducted from that person's total, and you continue until someone properly yells *Piggy!*)

10. The person with the highest score for each game advances to the next table, and the loser from table 1 starts back at the last table. (Number your tables 1,2,3,4, etc.)

11. The game continues in this fashion until the total of ten games are completed. (You may shorten the number of games if you wish.)

12. Have all players total all the games to arrive at the grand total.

13. Have door prizes for the winner and loser. Select appropriate prizes that relate to pigs—e.g., sausage, bacon, corn, etc.

14. HAVE A GREAT EVENING OF FUN!

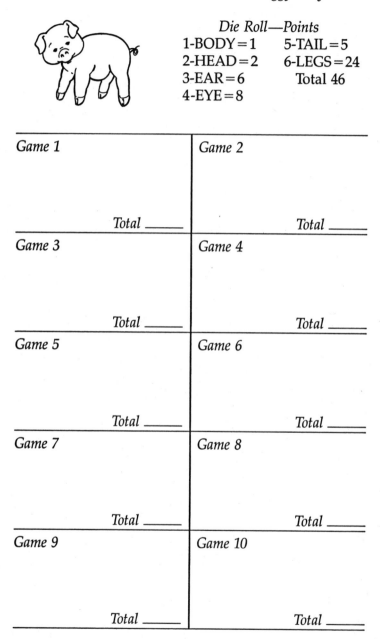

Die Roll—Points
1-BODY = 1   5-TAIL = 5
2-HEAD = 2   6-LEGS = 24
3-EAR = 6   Total 46
4-EYE = 8

Game 1	Game 2
Total _____	Total _____
Game 3	Game 4
Total _____	Total _____
Game 5	Game 6
Total _____	Total _____
Game 7	Game 8
Total _____	Total _____
Game 9	Game 10
Total _____	Total _____

Part

5

*More Hours . . .
for Your Children*

36

Children Need to Be Organized, Too

*Train a child in the way
he should go, and when he is old
he will not turn from it.*

Proverbs 22:6, NIV

❧ —— ❧

I can remember when Brad and Jenny were young and I can say that these were difficult times in my life because their ideas and my ideas of organization were different—like North Pole and South Pole.

However, there are a few ideas that did work, and I'm sure they will work for you, too. Remember: This period of your life and theirs doesn't last for more than a few years. It passes soon, and now there are many days when I walk down the hall and wish I could look into their rooms and find a crooked bedspread. They aren't living at home anymore, and I can truthfully say I miss those days of clutter. I can report that both of our children are grown, and in many areas they are more organized than I am. They were listening and watching during those tense years.

- Keep those socks sorted by pinning them together with a safety pin or clipping them together with clothes pins. Put the child's initials on the socks with a black paint pen.

- Review the family calendar together. On Sunday evening we would go over our large desktop calendar to see where we were all going to be during the coming week. Were there any transportation or babysitting needs—any church activities, birthday parties, holidays, etc.? Is all homework ready for Monday at school? Any gifts needed for the week? This let us touch bases and make sure we were all on the same schedule.

- Have one area where the children place all their school items. I used colored bins by the front door where each child would put his/her gym clothes, homework, schoolbooks. This saved a lot of last-minute hunting for items before running off to school.

- Have a dress-up box available for those spontaneous plays that your children perform on days they play inside because of weather. Today I use these old clothes for the grandchildren when they come over to play.

- Have a box of games, toys, and coloring books to take with you on long trips. Also bring along an old sheet and spread it on the backseat and floor. Let all the debris fall on the sheet. When you get to your destination, all you have to do is pull out the sheet, shake it on the ground, and put it back in the car.

- Some rooms can be off-limits, if you desire. This is an area of disagreement among parents, but we each have off-limit areas. That special area of yours can be off-limits until the children get to a certain age. I have a very valuable collection of china cups and saucers. The grandchildren know that those shelves are off-limits, but one day they will be able to touch and pick up the china.

- Color-code your children. Jenny knew that the yellow towels were hers, and Brad knew that his were blue. This color system can be used in many other assorted areas of the home.

- Make sure that each child has a place to hang clothes and store belongings. This place doesn't have to be expensive. Many times plastic bins and wooden crates work fine.

- Put the van Gogh artwork of your young artist on the refrigerator, bulletin board, or in a folder designated for that child's age or grade in school. Some of the extra artwork can be used in wrapping grandparents' gifts.

- Clean out a bedroom before the arrival of new items. Before birthdays, Christmas, and the change of seasons, go through the bedroom with the child assisting and help clean out old clothes, broken toys, and clothes that are too small. Be sure to use my three-bag system: 1) Give Away, 2) Put Away, and 3) Throw away. Reread the chapter "Total Mess to Total Rest." Give obsolete items to friends, neighbors, or church groups.

- Children need shelves, hooks, and bins. Let the children help decide where these items should be placed in the room.

- Each room needs a bulletin board to store all those pictures, awards, certificates, postcards, and special items.

- Each child needs to have a study center. Make sure there is plenty of light, basic supplies of pencils, pens, paper, paper clips, a stapler, ruler, hole punch, rubber bands. If this isn't possible, put all these items into a color-coded plastic bin where he/she can carry them to an area where homework can be done.

- Make sure you have a list of emergency numbers by the telephone. When going out for the evening, review with the children and their babysitter where you are going along with a phone number, and be sure to tell them the approximate time you will be home.

Be sensitive to your children's needs. Remember that they too have to have proper tools with which to be organized.

37

Safety Tips for School-Bound Children

*Better the little that the righteous have
than the wealth of many wicked; for the
power of the wicked will be broken,
but the Lord upholds the righteous.*

Psalm 37:16,17, NIV

èa ——— èa

As our children were growing up and going to
school, I never was concerned about their
safety as they went from home to school and
back again to home. We had neighborhood schools, we
all knew each other, and we lived in a kinder world. But
over the last ten years our culture has caused us to be
more and more conscious of safety for our children in all
situations.

The following school transportation safety tips could
save your child's life.

Here Comes the Yellow Bus

With more and more children taking the bus to school
for various reasons, teach your children to:

- Remain seated and keep the aisles clear.
- Not throw objects.
- Not make loud noises or distract the driver.

• Keep arms, head, and legs inside the bus.
• Wait for the bus to stop before exiting.
• Make sure they get on the correct bus.
• Help new riders out so they feel welcomed to the new school.

Riding That Bicycle to School

If your children ride bikes to school, make sure they are at least eight years old and teach them to:

• Choose a safe route, which may not be the same as a safe walking route. Young bicyclists should stay away from busy streets.
• Wear a helmet each time they ride their bicycle.
• Keep their bicycle in good working order. Fix any parts that aren't working properly. Keep the correct air pressure in the tires.
• Avoid night bicycle riding. Darkness drastically increases the chances of having an injury.
• Insist on only one rider per bicycle unless it is built for multiple riders.
• Store the bicycles in an enclosed area away from traffic.

Mom's Driving Me to School

• Make sure all children use their seat belts.
• Remove any heavy or loose objects that could become airborne if you were in an accident.
• Let children out of your car on the sidewalk on the school side of the street. Try to avoid having them cross a street to get to school.

- Pick children up at a safe place away from the congested area of cars.

- If carpooling, take added safety cautions. Remember: You are carrying someone else's most-prized possessions.

A Good Walk Will Do Them Good

- Walking is great exercise, and children have good, young, strong legs.

- Choose the safest route for your child before the first day of school. Try to choose the most direct route with the fewest street crossings. Let the child try a couple of dry runs on his own before that first day.

- Have your children take a familiar route to school each day, and encourage them to be consistent in their trip.

- Warn your children to not become distracted by strangers and to not go up to any strangers who might stop wanting information. It's better for children to be rude in this area and remain safe.

- Teach your children about all traffic markings. Explain the different color of lights and all signs. Even though the lights flash green, teach your children to look both ways before stepping out in the street.

- Teach your children to always use pedestrian crosswalks when crossing a street (if there are crosswalks).

- Warn your children to not cross a street between parked cars or behind buses.

- Warn your children to look left, right, and then left again before crossing the street.

To receive the booklet "How to Protect Your Child from Injury," send one dollar to National SAFE KIDS Campaign, Department BHG, 111 Michigan AV, NW—SK1, Washington, DC 20010.

38

Resolutions for Parenting

When times are good, be happy;
but when times are bad,
consider: God has made the one
as well as the other.

Ecclesiastes 7:14, NIV

❧ —— ❧

There are two times of the year when we write down resolutions for the new year:

- New Year's Day
- The beginning of school for our children.

Remember, you have already finished school once. It's your children who are going to school, not you. These resolutions include:

- Don't let children watch TV or play video games on school nights (at least until *all* their homework is completed). These activities waste a lot of creative time.

- Don't let feelings of inadequacy creep up on you because your children aren't doing well in a certain subject, or even the whole grade. The responsibility is upon the child; however, you do need to support and encourage the learning process.

315

- Homework is not yours—it's for your children. This is the most difficult of all the resolutions. Provide an adequate study area with proper light and space. Let them know you are available to help when absolutely needed. Their responsibility is to do their homework on a timely basis. While he or she is studying, protect your child from distractions such as loud noises, interruptions, TV, and visitors. Support your child's schoolteacher by making sure the work is done on time.

- Don't bail your children out when they leave their lunch and books at home—or vice versa, when they leave their books at school. It only takes a couple times of forgetting and they get the idea that it's their responsibility.

- Don't do large projects for your children. It's okay to help, but it's their responsibility to research and complete the project.

- Support your child's teacher. It's so important that your child realizes that you are supporting his or her teacher. If you have a difference of opinion with the teacher, set up an appointment.

- Let your children solve their own social problems, unless the situation is extraordinary. (With the increase in violence in our schools, this may not always be an easy resolution to keep.) Children need to learn to work out their own differences.

- You teach your 3 r's at home (respect, responsibility, resourcefulness) and let the teacher teach his/hers (reading, writing, and arithmetic). We need to send children to school who are ready to learn.

• Don't push your children into your areas of interest, but wait until they are ready and express a desire to participate. Today children are over-scheduled with outside activities. It becomes a real drain on the children's energy, but it also becomes a real drain on the parents' free time.

• Let your children grow and excel in the gifts that God has given them. Most children can't be good in all subjects or be interested in all outside activities. Let them excel in their strengths.

• Let your children know that you're on their team. Show a positive interest in your children's school activities. School can do a better job of teaching your children if teachers know you are interested in your children's learning. Teachers cry out, "Where are the interested parents?"

39

Jobs Children Can Do

*Children are a gift from God;
they are his reward.*

Psalm 127:3

≈ —— ≈

Delegating responsibility to children is such an important aspect of motherhood that you should be giving your children responsibilities at a very young age. Make it fun for them; make games out of it. A three-year-old can dress himself, put his pajamas away, brush his hair, brush his teeth, and make his bed. You can begin to teach your children these things when they're as young as two and three years old. Some more examples: folding clothes, emptying the dishwasher (they may need some help with that—begin by having them unload some of the plastic things), clearing some of the dishes off the table (begin by teaching them to carry things back into the kitchen), emptying wastebaskets, or picking up toys before bedtime (plastic baskets are excellent for toys).

Our Responsibility

Proverbs 22:6 (NASB) says, "Train up a child in the way he should go, even when he is old he will not depart from it." It is our responsibility as Christian parents to train our children and direct them and guide them in the ways that they should go, so that when they become adults they're not domestic invalids. It's important that we give our children responsibilities and train them up. A five-year-old can set the table, clean the bathrooms, and help clean and straighten drawers and closets. As you go through your home, take your little one with you and begin to show him what you're doing. Often children don't even realize that there's toothpaste on the mirror in the bathroom because they've never been told that they have to wipe it up. They think it just somehow automatically disappears.

Here are some more things children can do: clean up after the pet, feed the cat, walk the dog, dust the furniture. They may do a sloppy job of dusting, and you may say you'll just have to go back and do it over, but don't go back and do it until tomorrow. Let them move the dust around a little so they at least can see the responsibilities that their moms are fulfilling. Many of you work outside your home, then have to do a full-time job at home. You need to delegate these responsibilities to your children.

Seven and Up

Seven-year-olds can empty garbage, sweep walks, help in the kitchen after dinner, and prepare lunches for school. (If a child makes his own lunch, he's not too likely to complain about it!) Then have them help clean out the car. Don't forget that they're making messes in the car as you're driving them around. You'll find that when their friends get in the car and your children are the ones that have to clean up the car they'll say to their friends, "We don't drop things in our car."

A seven-year-old can begin to learn to iron. When our

daughter, Jenny, was eight years old she was doing all the laundry in our home, from washing it to putting it in the dryer (or hanging it up) to folding it. These are things that children can learn to do. It even helps their physical coordination to learn how to do these things.

An eight-year-old can learn to wash the bathroom mirrors, wash the windows, wash the floors in small areas, and polish shoes. As the children grow older they can be given more and more responsibilities, such as washing the car, mowing the lawn, making the dessert, painting, and cleaning the refrigerator.

When our children were growing up, we would delegate to each of them one night a week when they would completely prepare that meal. It could be their choice or it could be on the Menu Planner, but they were to completely make the meal. If you do this, you'll find that your children can be creative when you didn't even know they had it in them.

Teaching Our Children

Deuteronomy 6:5-7 (NASB) says, "You shall love the LORD your God with all your heart and with all your soul and with all your might. And these words, which I am commanding you today, shall be on your heart; and you shall teach them diligently to your sons and shall talk of them when you sit in your house and when you walk by the way and when you lie down and when you rise up." It is our responsibility as parents to be teaching our children in all areas—to teach them as we're in the kitchen, to teach them about God's creation when we're bicycling together, to teach them how to make a lunch and to picnic, or to teach them as we're at the park or the beach. We're to teach them many things as we build our home around our family, and as we organize and become creative.

We by ourselves cannot do it all in our homes (when we try, we become frustrated), so when we begin to delegate responsibilities to our children and allow them to do some of the work for us, they begin to feel as if they are a vital part of the family. I have found that families that work together and play together will also love together, pray together, and worship God together. Then we'll raise children who are balanced people, who will become creative adults with wonderful homes of their own.

JOBS FOR YOUR CHILDREN

Three-year-old

1. Get dressed, put pajamas away
2. Brush hair
3. Brush teeth
4. Make bed
5. Fold clothes and small items
6. Empty dishwasher (will need help with this)
7. Clear meal dishes
8. Empty wastebaskets
9. Pick up toys before bed

Five-year-old

1. Set table
2. Clean bathroom sink
3. Help clean and straighten drawers and closets
4. Clean up after pet
5. Feed pet
6. Walk dog
7. Dust furniture in room
8. Vacuum room
9. Help put groceries away

Seven-year-old

1. Empty garbage
2. Sweep walks
3. Help in kitchen after dinner
4. Help make lunch for school
5. Do schoolwork
6. Clean out car
7. Take piano lessons, etc.
8. Iron flat items

Eight-year-old

1. Wash bathroom mirrors
2. Wash windows
3. Wash floors in small area
4. Polish shoes

As your children grow, more responsibilty can be given to them:

1. Wash car
2. Mow lawn
3. Make dessert
4. Paint
5. Clean refrigerator
6. Do yard work
7. Iron
8. Fix an entire meal
9. Do grocery shopping

Children need to know they are valuable to the family and they are needed in order for the family to function properly. It is easier for children to have a positive attitude toward themselves when they are around people who believe in their worth. Children want to help and to feel needed, and they want to do important jobs. The outcome of the job is not as important as helping a child develop skills and capabilities.

What we need to do as parents is to take time to train our children. Whenever we appreciate their contributions, no matter how small, we are helping them to see themselves as capable people.

HELPFUL HINTS

- *From a creative mother:* After many nights of interrupted sleep, I finally hit on a solution that keeps my five-year-old in her own bed—at least most nights. I labeled one bowl "Mama's Bed Buttons" and another "Christine's Bed Buttons" and put 25 small buttons in each. For every night Christine stays in bed, I owe her one button. She pays me a button if she gets in bed with me. When her bowl is filled, we do something special—a roller-skating trip, a movie, an outing of her choice. Now she only comes to my bed if she really feels she has to.

- One most-appreciated gift a neighbor gave me after the birth of my first baby was a freshly baked apple pie with a card attached worth eight hours of free babysitting. The pie hit the spot, since I was tired of eating all that hospital food, and it was reassuring to know there was someone available close by to babysit if needed.

- Once a year, I have a babysitter swap party. Each attendee must bring the names and telephone numbers of three reliable sitters.

- A tasty variation on the standard peanut-butter-and-jelly sandwich: Make the sandwich as usual, but just before serving, butter the outside of the bread, and brown the sandwich in a hot skillet.

- When sewing buttons on children's clothing, use elastic thread. It makes buttoning much simpler for little fingers.

- Here is a little idea for young children at a fast-food store or restaurant. When you buy the tot a soft drink, cut the straw off short so it is easier to hold and drink. There is less chance of a child spilling or dropping the drink, too.

40

How to Teach Your Children About Money

*For the man who uses well
what he is given shall be given more,
and he shall have abundance.*

Matthew 25:29

ॐ ——— ॐ

We live in a world where adults find themselves in financial woes. Where do we learn about money? Usually by trial and error. Few families take the time to teach their children how to be smart with money. At an early age, children need to know about money and what it can do for them.

Children who learn about money at an early age will be ahead of this mystery game. Learning to deal with money properly will foster discipline, good work habits, and self-respect.

Below you will find several ways you can help your children get a good handle on money.

1. *Start with an allowance.* Most experts advise that an allowance should not be tied directly to a child's daily chores. Children should help around the home not because they get paid for it, but because they share responsibilities as members of a family. However, you might pay children for doing extra jobs at home. This can develop their initiative. We know of parents who give

stickers to their children when the children do a chore they haven't been asked to do. At the children's discretion, they may redeem the stickers for 25 cents each. This has been a great motivator not only for initiative but for teaching teamwork in the family.

An allowance is a vital tool for teaching children how to budget, save, and make their own decisions. Children remember and learn from mistakes when their own money is lost or spent foolishly.

How large of an allowance you give your children depends upon your individual status. It should be based upon developing a fair budget that allows for entertainment, snacks, lunch money, bus fare, and school supplies. Add some extra money for the church and savings. Be willing to hold your children responsible for living within their budget. Some weeks they may have to go without when they run out of money.

2. *Model the proper use of credit.* In today's society we see the results of individuals and couples using bad judgment regarding credit. Explain to children why it's necessary to use credit and the importance of paying their loan back on a timely basis. You can make this a great teaching tool. Give them practice in filling out credit forms. Their first loan might be from you to them for a special purchase. Go through all the mechanics that a bank would do: Have them fill out a credit application and sign a paper with all the information stated. Let them understand about interest, installment payments, balloon payments, late-payment costs, etc. Teach them to be responsible about paying on time.

3. *Teach your children how to save.* In today's instant society, it is hard to teach this lesson. At times we should deny our children certain material things so they have a reason to save. As they get older they will want bicycles,

stereos, a car, a big trip, etc. They can relate to establishing the habit of saving with these larger items.

One of the first ways to begin teaching the concept of savings is to give the children a form of piggy bank. This way spare change or extra earnings can go into the piggy bank. When the bank gets full, you might want to open an account for them at the local bank.

When they are older, you might want to establish a passbook account at the local bank so they can go to the bank and personally deposit in their account. Most banks will not pay interest until the balance becomes larger, but this helps the children begin thinking about savings.

In the end, children who learn how to handle money will better appreciate what they've worked to acquire.

4. *Show them how to be wise in their spending.* Take your children with you when you shop and do some cost comparisons. They will soon see that with a little effort they can save a lot of money. You might want to show them in a tangible way when they want to purchase a larger item for themselves. Go to several stores looking for that one item and write down the most expensive price and the least amount for the same item. Let them choose which one they want to purchase, and pay them the difference between what they chose and the most expensive. This way they can really see the savings.

Clothes is an area where a lot of lessons on wise spending can be made. After a while children realize that designer clothes cost a lot more for just that label or patch. Our daughter, Jenny, soon learned that outlet stores were great bargains for clothes dollars. To this day she can still find excellent bargains by comparison shopping.

5. *Let children work part-time.* There are many excellent part-time jobs waiting for your child. Fast-food outlets,

markets, malls, babysitting, etc., give valuable work experience to your children. Some entrepreneurial youngsters even begin a thriving business around their skills and interest. These part-time jobs are real confidence boosters. Just remember to help them keep a proper balance between work, home, church, and school. A limit of 10-15 hours per week might be a good guideline. Much more than that will affect a proper balance.

6. *Let them help you with your expenses.* Encourage your children to help you budget the family finances and pay for expenses. This gives them experience in real-life money problems. They also get a better idea regarding your family's financial income and expenses. Children's ideas are good when it comes to suggestions about how we can better utilize the family finances. This will give them a better understanding of why your family can't afford certain luxuries.

7. *Give them experience in handling adult expenses.* As your children get older, they need to experience real-life costs. Since children live at home, they don't always share in true-to-life expenses. Let them experience paying for their own telephone, car, and clothing expenses. Depending upon the situation, help in paying a portion of the utility and household bills would be an invaluable experience for children who have left school and are still living at home.

8. *Give unto the Lord.* At a very young stage in life, parents and children should talk about where things come from. The children should be aware that all things are given by God and He is just letting us borrow them for a time. Children can understand that we are to return back to God a portion of what He has so abundantly given to us. This principle can be experienced either through their Sunday school or church offerings. When

special projects at church come up, you might want to review the need with your children so they can decide if they want to give extra monies above what they normally give to their church. Early training in this area gives a valuable basis for learning how to be a giver in life and not a taker.

Your children will learn about money from you. Be a good model. As they get older, they will imitate what you do. If you have good habits, they will reflect that; if you struggle with finances, so will they. One valuable lesson to teach is that money doesn't reflect love, and that it is not a payoff for the children. A hug, a smile, a kiss, or time spent together is much more valuable than money.

41

Children Can Travel Alone

Listen, my sons, to a father's instruction;
pay attention and gain understanding.

Proverbs 4:1, NIV

è&. —— è&.

As our society becomes more travel-conscious and as more and more families live apart from each other geographically, it isn't uncommon to have children travel alone by air, bus, and train. If you're sending a child on a long trip, you should know and follow the rules set by these various companies.

Airlines

Most U.S. carriers do not accept children under five years old traveling alone. Check with your preferred carrier regarding its limits. As a general rule, unaccompanied children ages five to seven can travel only on direct, nonstop flights. For children ages eight to eleven, most airlines require an escort to take the children between connecting flights for a nominal fee of $25 to $30 each way.

When you book your flight, be sure to tell the agent that you are booking an unaccompanied minor. Also request a child's meal, which must be reserved six to twenty-four hours ahead of departure time. Take your child to the airport at least one hour before the plane is scheduled to leave. Don't add stress by being short on time. Allow for an emergency—and maybe even for getting lost.

You must complete an identification form at the ticket counter, naming the adult who will pick up your child on arrival. That person must present proper identification (a photo ID is best) before airline personnel will release your child.

Make sure that your child has a secure way to carry tickets, ID cards, and pocket money for minor purchases such as in-flight headsets. Pack healthful snacks, even if you have ordered the child's meal. Dress your child in layered clothing so he can add or remove clothes, depending on cabin temperature. The flight attendant can provide your child with pillows and light blankets.

Provide quiet, clean activities to keep your child occupied during the flight. While electronic games and devices are allowed, they must be relatively quiet. Devices that send or receive signals (e.g., a remote-controlled toy or radio) are not allowed.

I have found in my travels that the general public go out of their way to be nice and helpful to children who are traveling alone.

Bus Companies

The nation's largest bus line, Greyhound, allows children who are at least eight years old to travel as unaccompanied minors. However, younger children may travel with a companion who is at least 12 years old. They must travel during the daytime, on trips lasting no longer than five hours that require no change of bus. The trip must end at a full-service Greyhound terminal.

When you take your child to the terminal, you must complete an identification form and take the child to the customer-service manager, who will then escort the child onto the bus. During the trip, the bus driver will assume responsibility for the child.

It is recommended that you pack snacks and provide activities to keep your child busy. Earphones are required for radios, tape players, and electronic devices.

The adult picking up the child must present identification and sign a release form at the terminal where the trip ends.

Trains

This mode of travel has stricter requirements than other means. Because trains can carry a larger number of travelers with many more stops along a given route, Amtrak enforces stricter rules.

Children must be at least eight years old to travel alone. In most cases an Amtrak representative will interview children between eight and eleven years old to see if they are mature enough for traveling alone. They can only travel during daylight hours with no change of trains.

For added protection you might want to consider a one-person sleeping car. This added protection will be more expensive than a regular ticket (in some cases it is double the cost). Sleeping cars have compartments that lock, and a full-time porter is assigned to each car.

No matter which way your child will travel, it is good to plan ahead. All forms of transportation are relatively safe, and each company goes to great lengths to make traveling a safe and pleasant experience for your child.

Appendix
Notes

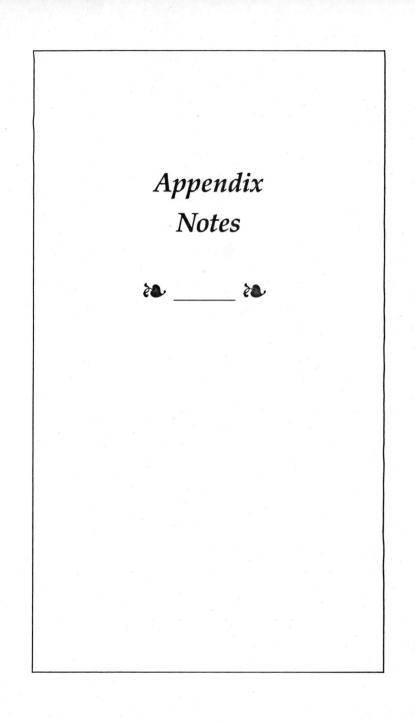

Appendix

*Be beautiful inside, in your hearts, with the
lasting charm of a gentle and quiet spirit
which is so precious to God.*

1 Peter 3:4

ॐ —— ॐ

Sample Daily Routine

A. *Start your day the night before.*

**"She is energetic, a hard worker, and watches
for bargains. She works far into the night."**
(Proverbs 31:17,18)

- Gather, sort, and wash laundry.
- Set the breakfast table.
- Lay out vitamins in individual cups.
- Set up coffeepot for the morning.
- Make a "To Do" list of what must be done the
  next day.

B. *Get up early.*

**"She gets up before dawn to prepare breakfast
for her household, and plans the day's
work for her servant girls."**
(Proverbs 31:15)

- Make the bed, one side at a time.

- Put on a decent robe or attractive clothes.
- Do at least a light makeup job and hair combing.
- Put in the first load of wash.

C. *Advance to the kitchen.*

> **"She watches carefully all that goes on**
> **through out her household, and is never lazy."**
> (Proverbs 31:27)

- Rejoice that the table is set and attractive.
- Cook breakfast and put out butter, milk, etc.
- Call everyone to the table with a two-minute warning.
- Serve everyone at once and sit down yourself. (Don't be a short-order cook.)
- Remind everyone to take vitamins.
- Review each person's day, noting where you are needed.
- Have everyone take their dishes to the sink.
- Put all dishes in the sink to soak in hot water.
- Quickly put away all perishables.

D. *Say farewell to the family.*

> **"When she speaks, her words are wise, and**
> **kindness is the rule for everything she says."**
> (Proverbs 31:26)

- See if your husband has any needs.
- Check each child's room with him or her.
- See that the bed is made and clothes are hung up or in the wash.
- Check the bathroom for dirty clothes and for cleanliness.
- Check to see that each child has a lunch, money, books, homework, gym clothes, etc.
- Compliment them on how well they have done something.

- Send them off with a loving hug.
- Help them to remember you as a smiling mother and not as a screaming shrew.

Remember, "It's not what you expect, but what you inspect."

E. *Get back to work.*

> *"She is energetic, a hard worker."*
> (Proverbs 31:17)

- Put in a second load of wash.
- Do the dishes.
- Do any advance dinner preparation—brown hamburger for casserole, cook rest of bacon for future use, make a dessert, prepare Jell-O, etc.
- Clean up the counters.
- Water the houseplants.
- Do general housecleaning for 15 minutes a day in some area of your home.
- Rejoice that your basic housework is done and it's only nine o'clock!

F. *Prepare the home for the evening.*

> *"She watches carefully all that goes on through out her household, and is never lazy. Her children stand and bless her; so does her husband. He praises her with these words: 'There are many fine women in the world, but you are the best of them all!'"*
> (Proverbs 31:27-29)

- Light a fire and candles (seasonal).
- Prepare munchies if dinner is a bit late: energy mix, raisins and nuts, sour cream and cottage cheese dip with carrot sticks, cucumber, zucchini, or cauliflower.

- Set the table with a centerpiece.
- Prepare yourself: freshen your makeup, check your dress, check your hair, put on perfume.
- Start thinking toward a quiet and gentle spirit.
- Organize the children as best as you possibly can.
- Be ready for your husband's arrival.
- Always meet him. Get yourself up and to the door with a hug, kiss, and a smile.
- Let him have 15 minutes to unwind with the paper or the mail.
- Do not share the negative part of the day with him until after dinner.
- Enjoy your family.

For more information regarding speaking engagements and additional material on More
Hours in My Day, please send a self-addressed,
stamped envelope to:

More Hours in My Day
2838 Rumsey Drive
Riverside, CA 92506
(909) 682-4714
FAX: (909) 682-6224

Notes

Chapter 11—Feel Safe When You Travel
1. Peter A. Dickinson, ed., *The Retirement Letter* (mid-Dec. 1993), issue 323, pp. 5-8.

Chapter 22—Dollar Mistakes to Avoid
1. Bob and Emilie Barnes, *The 15-Minute Money Manager* (Eugene, OR: Harvest House Publishers, 1993), pp. 53-58.
2. Barbara Gilder Quint, "Are You Throwing Your Money Away?" *Family Circle Magazine*, Sep. 21, 1993, p. 29.

Chapter 31—A Team Effort Starts at Home
1. Emilie Barnes, *Survival for Busy Women* (Harvest House Publishers, 1988), pp. 195-201.
2. Jay Adams, *Christian Living in the Home* (Baker Book House, 1972), pp. 91-92.
3. Bob and Emilie Barnes, *Growing a Great Marriage* (Harvest House Publishers, 1988), p. 27.

Chapter 40—How to Teach Your Children About Money
1. Bob and Emilie Barnes, *The 15-Minute Money Manager* (Eugene, OR: Harvest House Publishers, 1993).

Other Good
Harvest House Reading

SURVIVAL FOR BUSY WOMEN
Establishing Efficient Home Management
by *Emilie Barnes*

A hands-on manual for establishing a more efficient home-management program. Over 25 charts and forms can be personalized to help you organize your home.

THE CREATIVE HOME ORGANIZER
by *Emilie Barnes*

Most of the stress we experience is caused by a lack of organization and can be eliminated with careful planning and timely tips. Bursting with fast and easy methods to save time and energy in your home, *The Creative Home Organizer* has helpful hints for every area of your home. You can learn how to manage a household economically and have fun while doing it! Emilie Barnes also authored *More Hours in My Day* and *Survival for Busy Women*.

THE 15-MINUTE MONEY MANAGER
by *Bob & Emilie Barnes*

At last, a money-management book for busy people! Watch your finances come into focus as you apply the authors' proven 15-minute principle: Invest a small amount of time and make a big difference. Sixty-two short, quick-reading chapters have hundreds of ready-to-use ideas that will help you manage your money.

THINGS HAPPEN WHEN WOMEN CARE
by *Emilie Barnes*

Things Happen When Women Care shows you how to carve out time for others by streamlining the details of daily living and home organization. This warm, insightful look at developing friendships and enlarging the boundaries of your personal ministry will give you the tools you need to start today on the great adventure of caring for others.

THE COMPLETE HOLIDAY ORGANIZER
by *Emilie Barnes*

The busy woman's answer to holiday planning, *The Complete Holiday Organizer* gives ideas and helpful hints to make celebration preparations easier. A brief history about each holiday will challenge you to begin your own family traditions and memories. A practical "how-to" book to help you get a handle on holiday organization.

THE 15-MINUTE ORGANIZER
by *Emilie Barnes*

The 15-Minute Organizer is a dream book for the hurried and harried. Its 80 chapters are short and direct so you get right to the answers you need that will let you get ahead and stay ahead when the demands of life threaten to pull you behind.

YOUR HUSBAND, YOUR FRIEND
by *Bob Barnes*

It isn't easy to be a husband, spiritual leader, handyman, car repair expert, and chief spider killer all in one. Bob Barnes understands the inner fears and questions a man lives with. He gives wives an insider's look at a man's world and provides insights that noncommunicative husbands may not share.

15 MINUTES ALONE WITH GOD
by *Emilie Barnes*

Catch Emilie's heart as never before as she shares from the Bible. In warm, open devotions, Emilie shares her thoughts about praying for people, hospitality, encouragement, worry, grace, and other subjects close to heart and home. These daily meditations are written especially for busy women, providing encouragement and direction for the day from someone who's been there.

THE SPIRIT OF LOVELINESS
by *Emilie Barnes*

Join Emilie Barnes as she shares insights into the inner qualities of spiritual beauty and explores the places of the heart where true femininity is born. With hundreds of "lovely" ideas to help you personalize your home, Emilie shows that beauty *can* be achieved with even the lightest touch of creativity. Your spirit of loveliness will shine through as you make your home a place of prayer, peace, and pleasure for your family.

IF TEACUPS COULD TALK
by *Emilie Barnes*

Infused with the comforting atmosphere of a gentle afternoon tea, Emilie's newest book combines the nostalgic history of the English teatime with the welcoming spirit of hospitality. This charmingly illustrated book is a warm invitation to enjoy one of life's simple pleasures with one friend or several. For those wanting to learn the art of teatime, Emilie provides practical helps including directions for making perfect tea, suggestions for centerpieces and table coverings, and recipes for everything from scones to pinwheel sandwiches.